VERY
CHARLESTON

VERY CHARLESTON

A CELEBRATION OF HISTORY, CULTURE, AND LOWCOUNTRY CHARM

WRITTEN & ILLUSTRATED BY

DIANA HOLLINGSWORTH GESSLER

ALGONQUIN BOOKS OF CHAPEL HILL
2003

Published by
Algonquin Books of Chapel Hill
Post Office Box 2225
Chapel Hill, North Carolina 27515-2225

a division of
Workman Publishing
708 Broadway
New York, New York 10003

Library of Congress Cataloging-in-Publication Data
Gessler, Diana Hollingsworth, 1946–
Very Charleston : a celebration of history, culture,
and lowcountry charm / written and illustrated by
Diana Hollingsworth Gessler.— 1st ed.
p. cm.
Includes index.
ISBN 1-56512-339-5
1. Charleston (S.C.)—History—Miscellanea.
2. Charleston (S.C.)—History—Pictorial works.   I. Title.
F279.C457 G47 2003
975.7'915—dc21   2002033270

10   9   8   7   6   5   4
First Edition

In memory of my
aunt, Virginia Henley —
a very Charleston lady.

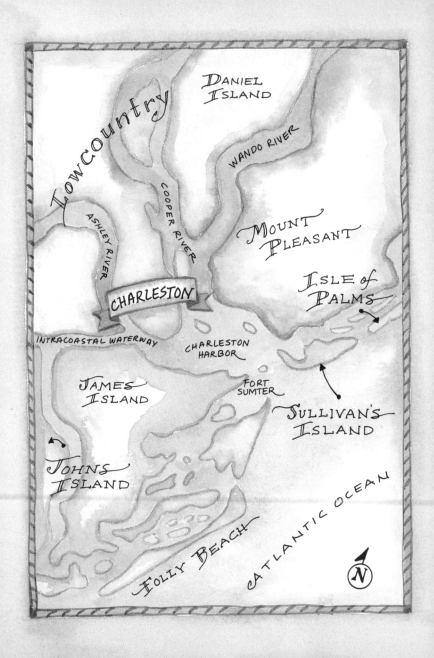

Crepe Myrtle trees along St. Michael's Alley

CONTENTS

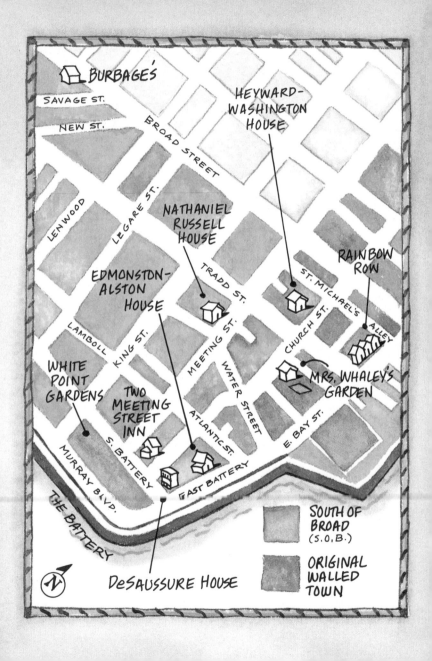

BURBAGE'S

SAVAGE ST.

NEW ST.

BROAD STREET

HEYWARD-WASHINGTON HOUSE

LENWOOD

LEGARE ST.

NATHANIEL RUSSELL HOUSE

RAINBOW ROW

ST. MICHAEL'S

EDMONSTON-ALSTON HOUSE

TRADD ST.

MEETING ST.

CHURCH ST.

ALLEY

LAMBOLL

KING ST.

WATER STREET

MRS. WHALEY'S GARDEN

WHITE POINT GARDENS

TWO MEETING STREET INN

ATLANTIC ST.

E. BAY ST.

S. BATTERY

MURRAY BLVD.

EAST BATTERY

THE BATTERY

DeSAUSSURE HOUSE

SOUTH OF BROAD (S.O.B.)

ORIGINAL WALLED TOWN

WINDOW DRESSING

CHAPTER 1

SOUTH OF BROAD

WHEN THE ENGLISH SAILED BY THIS PENINSULA IN 1670, THE TIP WAS MARSHY AND COVERED IN BLANCHED WHITE OYSTER SHELLS, WHICH IS WHY IT'S CALLED WHITE POINT.

THEY SETTLED UP THE ASHLEY RIVER IN CHARLES TOWNE. TEN YEARS LATER, DECIDING THAT THE POINT WOULD BE EASIER TO DEFEND & BETTER FOR TRADE, THEY MOVED TO THE EDGE OF THE MARSH. EVENTUALLY A WALL WAS BUILT AROUND THE TOWN. TODAY, MUCH OF THE AREA SOUTH OF BROAD IS "MADE LAND" (LANDFILL).

Charleston is my briar patch.

VIRGINIA OF TRADD STREET

THE BATTERY

White Point GARDENS

THINGS TO SEE IN THE PARK

PIGEON

"LITTLE DANCER"

DRINKING FOUNTAIN FOR CHILDREN & PIGEONS

USS HOBSON MEMORIAL

IN 1952, THE USS HOBSON COLLIDED WITH THE USS WASP WHILE TRAINING IN THE ATLANTIC. THE MEMORIAL HONORS THE MEN LOST WHEN THE HOBSON SANK IN 4 MINUTES.

KIDS CLIMBING CANNONBALLS

BLACK-EYED PEAS FED TO PIGEONS

WEDDINGS IN THE MEMORIAL BANDSTAND

CAST IRON "BATTERY" BENCHES FOUND ALL OVER TOWN

the De Saussure
HOUSE 1850

SECOND OWNER LOUIS DeSAUSSURE WAS LIVING HERE ON

APRIL 12, 1861 _at_ 3:30 A.M.

WHEN THE FIRST SHOTS OF THE CIVIL WAR WERE FIRED ON
FORT SUMTER. THE SHELLING CONTINUED FOR 34 HOURS.
DeSAUSSURE INVITED GUESTS TO GATHER ON THE ROOF
AND PIAZZAS OF THIS HOUSE WHERE THEY TOASTED AND
CHEERED THE "FIREWORKS".

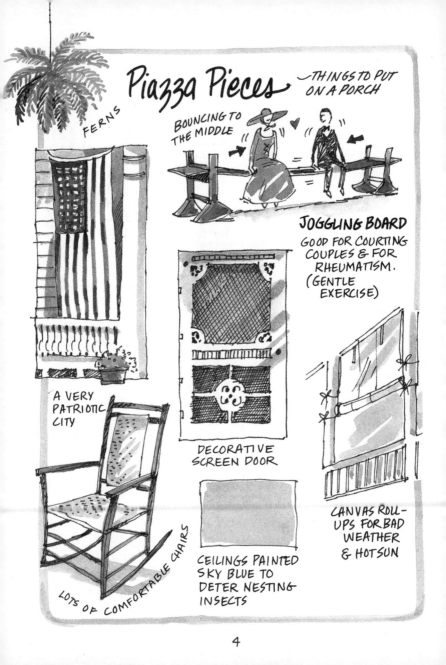

Piazza Pieces — THINGS TO PUT ON A PORCH

FERNS

BOUNCING TO THE MIDDLE

JOGGLING BOARD
GOOD FOR COURTING COUPLES & FOR RHEUMATISM. (GENTLE EXERCISE)

A VERY PATRIOTIC CITY

DECORATIVE SCREEN DOOR

LOTS OF COMFORTABLE CHAIRS

CEILINGS PAINTED SKY BLUE TO DETER NESTING INSECTS

CANVAS ROLL-UPS FOR BAD WEATHER & HOT SUN

4

EDMONDSTON-ALSTON HOUSE
1825

BUILT BY CHARLES EDMONDSTON FOR $25,000 AND SOLD TO CHARLES ALSTON FOR $15,500 AFTER THE PANIC OF 1837. THE ALSTON FAMILY STILL LIVES ON THE THIRD FLOOR.

HOUSE IS AMAZINGLY INTACT BECAUSE:

- IT HAS BOTH EXTERIOR AND INTERIOR SHUTTERS AND IS 2 BRICKS THICK.

- DAUGHTER SUSAN PRINGLE ALSTON SAVED EVERYTHING SO 90% IS ORIGINAL, INCLUDING FURNITURE AND FAMILY PAPERS.

ORIGINAL PAPER BAG WHERE ALL THE DEEDS & MORTGAGES WERE STORED.

Mammy's Bench

ON THE PIAZZA SO A "DAH" (MAMMY) COULD ROCK A BABY & STILL HAVE HANDS FREE TO SHELL BEANS!

5

Architectural Details

SLATE FROM WALES

PIAZZAS FACE SOUTH OR WEST FOR BREEZES.

PIAZZA FLOORS SLOPE DOWN FOR RAIN TO RUN OFF.

PRIVACY DOOR

YELLOW PINE OR CYPRESS CURED IN SALT WATER FOR HARDNESS. ROT & TERMITE RESISTANT.

EARTHQUAKE ROD COVERS

ONLY ONE ROOM WIDE

A CHARLESTON SINGLE HOUSE

FRONT FACES STREET.

© PRESERVATION SOCIETY OF CHARLESTON
AWARD
CAROLOPOLIS
CONDITA A.D. 1670
PRESERVATION SOCIETY OF CHARLESTON

THE AWARD GIVEN FOR EXCELLENCE IN EXTERIOR RESTORATION OF LOCAL BUILDINGS.

AFTER THE EARTHQUAKE OF 1886, HOMES WERE RETROFITTED WITH LONG METAL RODS RUNNING THE LENGTH OF THE BUILDING & CAPPED WITH ROD COVERS.

UNUSUAL ROD COVER AT THE ROPER MANSION

THIS BAND ON CHIMNEYS IS VERY CHARLESTON.

*T*HE ROPE IS AN ANCIENT CHINESE SYMBOL FOR "MERCHANT." CHARLESTON MERCHANTS HAD CARVED ROPE DESIGNS AROUND WINDOWS & DOORS.

FAUX FINISHES

BECAUSE STONE & MARBLE WEREN'T AVAILABLE IN THE LOWCOUNTRY, & MARBLE CRACKS IN THE HUMIDITY.

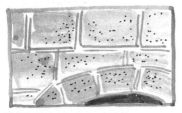

FAUX STONE: A BRICK BUILDING IS STUCCOED OVER & LINES ARE SCORED WHILE WET TO SIMULATE CUT STONE.

FAUX MARBLE: MARBLE-IZED PAPER IS CUT INTO RECTANGLES & MOUNTED ON THE WALL LIKE WALLPAPER.

*W*HEN DENMARK VESEY'S INSURRECTION AGAINST WHITES WAS ABORTED IN 1822, IRON SPIKES WERE ADDED TO THE FENCES OF WEALTHY CHARLESTONIANS LIKE MILES BREWTON'S HOUSE.

"CHEVAUX-de-FRISE"

"CHARLESTON GRAY BRICKS"— MADE LOCALLY—HAVE A BURNT LOOK.

7

"Charleston Green"

GREEN IS SO DARK IT LOOKS BLACK.

EXTERIOR GLOSS OIL-BASE PAINT

*A*FTER THE CIVIL WAR, THERE WAS LITTLE MONEY FOR SPRUCING THINGS UP. IT'S SAID THAT THE NORTH DONATED BLACK PAINT BUT LOCALS WERE HESITANT TO USE IT—AFTER ALL, IT <u>WAS</u> YANKEE PAINT.

THEY FOUND THAT MIXING 2 PARTS "YANKEE" BLACK & 1 PART "REBEL" YELLOW PRODUCED A DARK GREEN THAT HAS BECOME CHARLESTON'S SIGNATURE COLOR, ESPECIALLY FOR SHUTTERS.

EAST BAY STREET

Rainbow Row
1730-1750

9 HOUSE
COLORS FROM
NORTH TO
SOUTH →

*B*EFORE LANDFILL WAS ADDED, THESE MERCHANT STORES WERE ON THE WHARF. BACK THEN IT WAS A SEEDY, DANGEROUS PLACE.

IN THE 1920'S, PEOPLE BEGAN RESTORING THE RUN-DOWN BUILDINGS, PAINTING THE EXTERIORS IN PASTEL COLORS. THIS PROJECT LED TO THE RESTORATION OF THE REST OF CHARLESTON AND THE BIRTH OF THE CHARLESTON PRESERVATION SOCIETY— THE FIRST IN THE NATION.

Two Meeting Street Inn 1890

*A*CCORDING TO LEGEND, MARTHA WILLIAMS'S FATHER PRESENTED HER WITH A WEDDING GIFT OF $75,000 ON A SATIN PILLOW. THE YOUNG CARRINGTONS USED IT TO BUILD THIS QUEEN ANNE HOUSE.

Early Entertaining

MARROW SPOON

TO SCOOP THE MARROW OUT OF BONES

KNIFE BOX

HELD ALL SILVER-WARE—NOT JUST KNIVES.

TABLECLOTHS

TABLE WAS SET WITH MULTIPLE CLOTHS, EACH REMOVED AFTER A COURSE.

AFTER "THE LAST REMOVE," DESSERT WAS SERVED ON THE BARE TABLE.

WINE CELLARETTE

VERY POPULAR IN CHARLESTON. SOME HOMES HAD 3-5.

ENGLISH OR FRENCH CHINA

FOR ENTERTAINING. CHARLESTONIANS USUALLY HAD A PROCURING AGENT IN ENGLAND.

CHINESE IMPORT DISHES

BECAUSE COMPLETE SETS WERE SHIPPED IN BARRELS BY THE BOATLOAD AND SOLD AS IS AT THE WHARF, THEY WERE USED FOR EVERYDAY DINING.

The Pineapple Legend

THE SYMBOL OF HOSPITALITY COMES IN ALL SHAPES & SIZES.

WALKING AROUND CHARLESTON, YOU'LL SEE CARVED PINEAPPLES AT THE ENTRANCES TO SOME HOMES.

SINCE COLONIAL DAYS, THE PINEAPPLE HAS BEEN A SYMBOL OF HOSPITALITY.

LEGEND HAS IT THAT SEA CAPTAINS SAILING THE CARIBBEAN CAME HOME WITH EXOTIC FRUITS.

A CAPTAIN WOULD SPEAR A PINEAPPLE ON HIS FENCE POST TO LET FRIENDS KNOW HE WAS HOME SAFELY AND TO PLEASE VISIT. HE WOULD THEN SERVE FOOD & DRINK AND REGALE VISITORS WITH TALES OF THE HIGH SEAS.

THE NATHANIEL RUSSELL HOUSE 1808

*B*UILT FOR $80,000 BY "THE KING OF THE YANKEES," A RHODE ISLANDER WHO CAME HERE TO SEEK HIS FORTUNE. ONE OF THE GRANDEST HOMES IN AMERICA, THE GEOMETRICALLY SHAPED MAIN ROOMS INCLUDE TWO SQUARE, TWO RECTANGLE, AND TWO OVAL ROOMS.

RESTORERS HAVE CHIPPED THROUGH 22 LAYERS OF PAINT TO DISCOVER SUCH TREASURES AS MOLDINGS WITH TINY CARVED PINEAPPLES, GOLD TRIM, & FAUX FINISHES.

A SECTION OF THE BANISTER FROM THE "FLYING" STAIRCASE, WHICH SPIRALS UP SEEMINGLY UNSUPPORTED.

EACH PIECE OF WOOD IS CUT SEPARATELY — LIKE A PUZZLE.

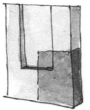

RESTORERS STRIPPED ALL PAINT OFF THIS DOOR, BUT LEFT A SMALL PATCH UNTOUCHED FOR FUTURE TECHNOLOGY TO ANALYZE.

THE ORIGINAL DINING ROOM COLOR!

DOORS & PANELS WERE ORIGINALLY FAUX PAINTED TO MIMIC FINE WOODS.

SOME PLINTH BLOCKS WERE FAUX PAINTED TO SIMULATE THE GEMSTONE LAPIS LAZULI.

Secret Gardens

WISTERIA

PEEK THROUGH A GARDEN GATE IN CHARLESTON AND YOU'LL FIND YET ANOTHER REASON FOR WANTING TO LIVE HERE— PERFECTLY PLANTED MAGICAL GARDENS TUCKED INTO SMALL SPACES.

Charleston
DREAM GARDEN

1. DIVIDED INTO GARDEN "ROOMS".
2. WATER IS SOOTHING.
3. POTTING SHED — CAMOUFLAGED.
4. PLAY "ROOM".
5. TREE "BORROWED" FROM NEIGHBOR.
6. PLACE TO READ & THINK.
7. COVER NEIGHBOR'S WALL.
8. PERENNIALS FOREVER GREEN.
9. ANNUALS — FOR CUTTING.
10. ALWAYS A STATUE.
11. SOMETHING CASCADING.
12. TREE HIDES TELEPHONE POLE.

FRONT ROW GARDEN SEAT

GIVE THEM A HOME...

LADY BANKSIA ROSES ENTWINED WITH PINK BUTTERFLY ROSES

...& A BATH.

Furnishing the Garden

ESSENTIALS

STATUETTE

A POTTING SHED VIGNETTE

A CHARLESTON ORNAMENTAL IRON WHEEL EMBEDDED IN A GARDEN GATE

DIFFERENT WALKWAYS:

WITH FLAGSTONE

"TABBY"

EARLY SETTLERS' TECHNIQUE: MIX OYSTER SHELLS, LIME, & SAND.

BALLAST STONES

Mr. Burbage's Grocery

BOILED PEANUTS

A "CORNER STORE" SINCE 1874 AND STILL SERVING THE NEIGHBORHOOD.

TODAY, ONLY A FEW ARE LEFT IN THE CITY.

Yes. We have filet mignon.

MR. BURBAGE

Mrs. Whaley's Garden

IN 1940, MRS. WHALEY ASKED FAMED LANDSCAPE ARCHITECT LOUTREL BRIGGS TO DESIGN HER GARDEN. HE CREATED "GARDEN ROOMS" BORDERED BY LOW HEDGES WITH A CENTER LAWN.

HIS PLAN WAS IN KEEPING WITH HER AUNT'S SAYING: "AN ENCLOSED GARDEN PUSHES BACK THE WILDERNESS AND KEEPS YOU SAFE FROM THE "HAINTS" (GULLAH FOR GHOSTS).

MRS. WHALEY PUBLISHED TWO BOOKS AND GENEROUSLY OPENED HER GARDEN TO THE PUBLIC ON CERTAIN OCCASIONS.

17

GEORGE WASHINGTON'S "Southern Tour"

PRESIDENT WASHINGTON KEPT AN INAUGURAL PROMISE TO VISIT THE SOUTH. HE TRAVELED BY CARRIAGE, BUT BEFORE EACH SCHEDULED STOP, HE MOUNTED HIS HORSE FOR A GRAND ENTRANCE.

MAY 2-9, 1791

HE ARRIVED AT MT. PLEASANT AND BOARDED A BARGE FOR CHARLESTON, LANDING AT THE END OF QUEEN STREET TO A FESTIVE RECEPTION—THE WHIRLWIND WEEK OF ENTERTAINMENT HAD BEGUN.

THE CITY RENTED HIM (AT HIS REQUEST, TO AVOID FAVORITISM) THE HEYWARD HOUSE, WHICH THEY STAFFED AND STOCKED.

FROM WASHINGTON'S JOURNAL

Went to a concert where were 400 ladies, the number and appearance of wch. exceeded anything I had ever seen.

G Washington

The
Heyward-Washington
HOUSE 1772

THOMAS HEYWARD Jr. WAS A SIGNER OF THE DECLARATION OF INDEPENDENCE. HIS FATHER BUILT THIS HOUSE AND GEORGE WASHINGTON SLEPT HERE — THUS THE NAME.

ELFE'S FRETWORK ON THE MANTLE

FIGURE 8

4 DIAMONDS

THOMAS ELFE WAS CHARLESTON'S BEST & MOST PROLIFIC CABINETMAKER. HE WORKED MOSTLY IN MAHOGANY & HIS "SIGNATURE" WAS A FIGURE 8 WITH 4 DIAMONDS.

A CHIPPENDALE CHAIR BY ELFE

CALLED A "CHEST ON CHEST ON CHEST." EACH CAN BE LIFTED OFF & PUT ON THE CARRIAGE FOR TRAVELING.

PERHAPS GEORGE LEFT THIS ON HIS VISIT.

BONE TOOTHBRUSH FOUND HERE.

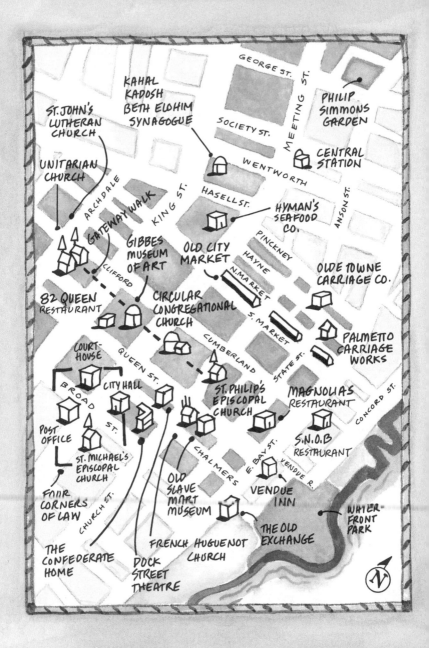

THE LIBRARY RESTAURANT AT VENDUE INN

CHAPTER 2

DOWNTOWN

CHARLESTON CALLS ITSELF THE "HOLY CITY" BECAUSE OF ITS MANY PLACES OF WORSHIP AND SKYLINE FULL OF CHURCH STEEPLES.

ABUNDANT, TOO, ARE RESTAURANTS & SOUTHERN SPECIALTIES. SAMPLE ENOUGH—ESPECIALLY SWEETS—AND IT'LL FEEL LIKE THE "HOLY ROLY POLY CITY".

BUT MOST OF ALL, THERE'S A LOT OF HISTORY. DOWNTOWN CHARLESTON WAS THE MEETING PLACE OF SOME OF AMERICA'S FIRST REVOLUTIONARY PATRIOTS.

COBBLESTONES ON CHALMERS ST.

MORE LIKE COBBLEROCKS!

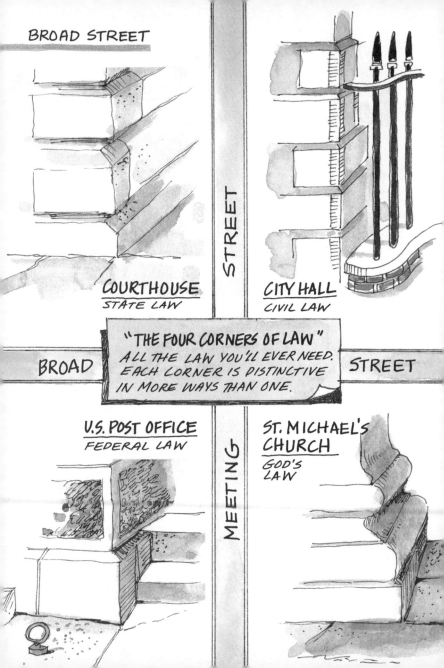

CHARLESTON COUNTY HISTORIC
Courthouse

1753: FIRST STATEHOUSE OF SOUTH CAROLINA. SEAT OF THE BRITISH GOVERNOR & COLONIAL ASSEMBLY.

1788: GUTTED BY FIRE.

1791: GEORGE WASHINGTON SAW LOCAL ARCHITECT JAMES HOBAN'S RESTORATION & ASKED HIM TO DESIGN THE WHITE HOUSE. STYLES ARE SIMILAR.

1792: BECAME A COURTHOUSE.

2001: REOPENED AFTER A 12-YEAR HOTLY DEBATED RESTORATION — WHETHER TO RETURN THE FAÇADE TO THE 1753 OR THE 1792 DESIGN.

1792 WON.

HOLDING THE KEYS TO THE COURTHOUSE, CLERK OF COURTS ANNOUNCES OFFICIAL REOPENING.

23

City Hall and the City Council Chamber

1818

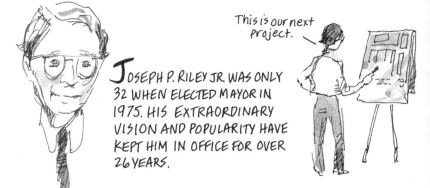

This is our next project.

J OSEPH P. RILEY JR. WAS ONLY 32 WHEN ELECTED MAYOR IN 1975. HIS EXTRAORDINARY VISION AND POPULARITY HAVE KEPT HIM IN OFFICE FOR OVER 26 YEARS.

AT THE CITY COUNCIL CHAMBER ACROSS FROM THE MAYOR'S OFFICE, MEMBERS STILL SIT AT THE ORIGINAL 1818 DESKS. DURING UNION OCCUPATION, THE COMMANDING GENERAL TOOK THE DESKS AND CHAIRS FOR HIS OFFICE. WHEN HE LEFT, ONLY THE DESKS WERE FOUND.

"NEW" SINCE 1870

NATIVE SOUTH CAROLINA BLACK WALNUT

Postal History Museum

IN THE POST OFFICE BUILDING
1896

SOUTH CAROLINA WAS THE FIRST TO SECEDE FROM THE UNION & THUS THE FEDERAL POSTAL SYSTEM.

SO THEY HAD TO PRINT THEIR OWN MONEY &

Postage Stamps. →

FIVE-CENT DAVIS

FIRST STAMP OF THE CONFEDERATE POSTAL SERVICE (1861) & THE FIRST TO PICTURE A LIVING AMERICAN — JEFFERSON DAVIS, PRESIDENT OF THE CONFEDERACY.

TEN-CENT DAVIS

WITHDRAWN AFTER IT WAS ISSUED IN 1863 — LOOKED TOO MUCH LIKE THAT OTHER PRESIDENT — MR. LINCOLN!

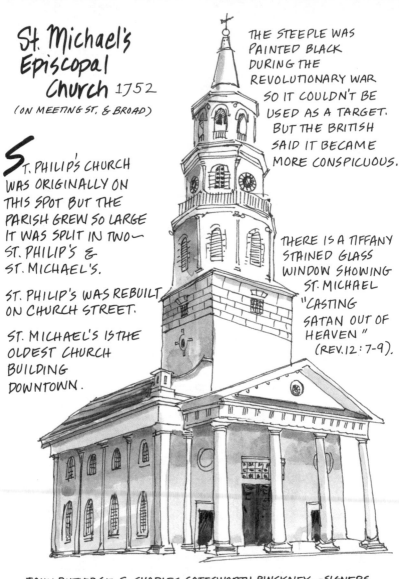

St. Michael's Episcopal Church 1752
(ON MEETING ST. & BROAD)

ST. PHILIP'S CHURCH WAS ORIGINALLY ON THIS SPOT BUT THE PARISH GREW SO LARGE IT WAS SPLIT IN TWO — ST. PHILIP'S & ST. MICHAEL'S.

ST. PHILIP'S WAS REBUILT ON CHURCH STREET.

ST. MICHAEL'S IS THE OLDEST CHURCH BUILDING DOWNTOWN.

THE STEEPLE WAS PAINTED BLACK DURING THE REVOLUTIONARY WAR SO IT COULDN'T BE USED AS A TARGET. BUT THE BRITISH SAID IT BECAME MORE CONSPICUOUS.

THERE IS A TIFFANY STAINED GLASS WINDOW SHOWING ST. MICHAEL "CASTING SATAN OUT OF HEAVEN" (REV. 12:7-9).

JOHN RUTLEDGE & CHARLES COTESWORTH PINCKNEY — SIGNERS OF THE U.S. CONSTITUTION — ARE BURIED HERE.

THESE WERE ONCE PRIVATE PEWS.

GEORGE WASHINGTON & ROBERT E. LEE WORSHIPED IN THE GOVERNOR'S PEW. OTHER VISITORS SAT IN A "LARGE PEW FOR STRANGERS."

KEYHOLES!

SEATS ONLY 15" WIDE!

KNEELING STOOL IS COMFORTABLE.

the BELLS of ST. MICHAEL'S
MADE 7 ATLANTIC VOYAGES!

1. 1764: SENT FROM WHITECHAPEL FOUNDRY, LONDON.
2. BRITISH HAULED THEM BACK AS A WAR PRIZE.
3. WERE RETURNED AFTER REVOLUTIONARY WAR.
4. DAMAGED DURING CIVIL WAR & SENT BACK TO WHITECHAPEL.
5. RECAST & RETURNED TO CHARLESTON.
6. 1989: DAMAGED BY HURRICANE HUGO & SENT BACK TO THE SAME FOUNDRY!
7. RETURNED TO CHARLESTON IN 1993.

RINGING OF THE BELLS

The Confederate Home 1867

After the Civil War, two sisters mortgaged their house to buy the "Carolina Hotel". They called it the "Home for the Mothers, Widows, and Daughters of Confederate Soldiers". These "permanent inmates" paid $1/month if able & were given soap 3 times a week.

SERVED WITH MINT

St. Michael's Church celebrated its 250th year in the courtyard garden & served a punch recipe from 1751.

THE OLD EXCHANGE &
PROVOST DUNGEON

PROVOST DUNGEON: WHERE THE BRITISH IMPRISONED AMERICAN PATRIOTS.

THE GREAT HALL: WHERE SOUTH CAROLINA'S DELEGATES TO THE CONTINENTAL CONGRESS WERE ELECTED AND WHERE WASHINGTON DANCED.

HAPPY ENDING: ALMOST RAZED FOR A GAS STATION IN 1913, THE DAUGHTERS OF THE AMERICAN REVOLUTION NOW OWN IT.

THESE CHARLESTONIANS SIGNED THE DECLARATION OF INDEPENDENCE—LATER, THREE DID TIME IN THE DUNGEON.

ARTHUR MIDDLETON

THOMAS HEYWARD JR.

EDWARD RUTLEDGE
(YOUNGEST SIGNER—26)

THOMAS LYNCH JR.

29

Gateway Walk

ALONG THE WAY

THE GARDEN CLUB PRESIDENT GOT THE IDEA FOR A CITY NATURE WALK AFTER A VISIT TO PARIS. LOUTREL BRIGGS DESIGNED IT IN 1930.

PHILADELPHIA ALLEY

ST. PHILIP'S EPISCOPAL CHURCH

CHURCH ST.

CIRCULAR CONGREGATIONAL CHURCH

ST. PHILIP'S STRANGERS CHURCH-YARD

UNITARIAN GRAVEYARD WILDFLOWERS

MEETING STREET

GIBBES MUSEUM OF ART

GOV. AIKEN GATES & PERSEPHONE FOUNTAIN

CHARLESTON LIBRARY SOCIETY

KING STREET

ST. JOHN'S LUTHERAN CHURCH

UNITARIAN CHURCH

ARCHDALE STREET

30

SIDE BY SIDE: A Study in Contrasts

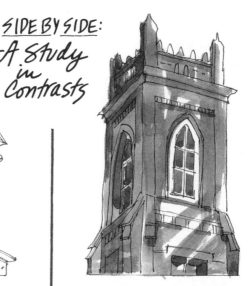

ST. JOHN'S LUTHERAN CHURCH 1817

A CRISP WHITE WEDDING-CAKE CHURCH PUNCTUATED WITH RED DOORS & SYMMETRICAL FLOORS.

UNITARIAN CHURCH 1780/ 1854

THE OVERGROWN GRAVE-YARD IS A TESTAMENT TO THE BELIEF THAT NATURE SHOULD REASSERT ITSELF.

CIRCULAR
CONGREGATIONAL CHURCH
1891

THIS INDEPENDENT CHURCH WAS FOUNDED BY SOME OF THE FIRST SETTLERS: ENGLISH CONGREGATIONALISTS, SCOTS PRESBYTERIANS, AND FRENCH HUGUENOTS. ALL MET ON THIS SITE AT <u>WHITE MEETING HOUSE</u>—THUS "MEETING STREET." IT HAS THE CITY'S OLDEST GRAVEYARD, DATING FROM 1696.

" **H**ere lies the bodies of three brothers...enwrapt in silence and the Arms of Death. Exposed to Worms lies three once charming Boys... "
1784

"IN THE SHADOW OF DEATH..."

ANGEL IS ABOUT TO RISE ABOVE DEATH.

Gibbes
Museum of Art
1905

As EARLY AS THE 1700'S, LIMNERS (TRAVELING ARTISTS) FLOCKED TO CHARLESTON. MANY WERE PORTRAIT PAINTERS LIKE SAMUEL MORSE, WHO EVENTUALLY THREW IN THE BRUSH AND INVENTED THE MORSE CODE.

VEILED LADY

1882
BY PIETRO ROSSI,
ITALIAN

THE VEIL SEEMS SO TRANSPARENT, IT'S HARD TO BELIEVE IT'S MARBLE.

GEORGE WASHINGTON

C. 1790
BY GIUSEPPE CERACCHI,
ITALIAN

THE MODE WAS TO MAKE CAESAR-LIKE BUSTS.

PERSEPHONE

1972
BY MARSHALL M. FREDERICKS,
AMERICAN

FOUNTAIN IN THE GARDEN — A NICE PLACE FOR A BROWN-BAG LUNCH.

HYMAN'S
SEAFOOD CO.

"A HYMAN ESTABLISHMENT SINCE 1890"

THIS IS THE PLACE WITH THE LONG LINE OUTSIDE—A FAVORITE OF LOCALS & MOVIE STARS.

FIFTH-GENERATION HYMAN TOBIAS PUTS BOILED PEANUTS ON THE TABLES.

PALMETTO BEER FROM LOCAL MICRO BREWERY • CRISPY FLOUNDER WITH HUSH PUPPIES

Hyman's Crab Dip

1 1/2 lbs. cream cheese
1/2 lb. cooked crabmeat
1/2 lb. small or diced cooked shrimp
3 tsp. horseradish
1/8 tsp. lemon juice

1/2 cup shredded cheddar cheese
2 tbsp. Hyman's Cajun Seasoning

Mix together and chill until firm.

Charleston Sweets

Cream-
Cheese
Brownie

Praline Soufflé
with Chocolate
Sauce

Benne Wafers —

Praline Candy

Sesame Seed Cookies - Very Charleston!

Crème
Brûlée

FRENCH HUGUENOT CHURCH
1845

WEDDING IN PROGRESS
— NO TOURS

THE ONLY INDEPENDENT
FRENCH CALVANIST
CONGREGATION
AND ONE OF THE LAST
TRACKER ORGANS
IN AMERICA.

BUILT OF BRICK &
COATED WITH
STUCCO. LACEY
IRON WORK
DEFINES THE
ROOFLINE &
WINDOWS.

CEMETERY SIGN

NON ENTRÉE

Festivals

Spoleto Festival
(LATE MAY – EARLY JUNE)
VISUAL & PERFORMING ARTS — AN ALL-YOU-CAN-SEE BUFFET.

JOSEPH FLUMMERFELT, DIR. WESTMINSTER CHOIR

I don't know how to weave sweet-grass baskets — I weave words.

Piccolo Spoleto
(SAME TIME AS SPOLETO)
"LITTLE SPOLETO" — LOCAL & REGIONAL PERFORMERS.

WESTMINSTER CHORALIER

MOJA Arts Festival
(LATE SEPTEMBER – EARLY OCTOBER)
CELEBRATION OF AFRICAN & CARIBBEAN CULTURAL ARTS.

GARDEN DOCENT

S.E. Wildlife Expo.
(FEBRUARY)
"LARGEST WILDLIFE EVENT IN THE COUNTRY"

POET DONNA SMITH

Festival of Houses & Gardens
(MID-MARCH — MID-APRIL)
SPONSORED BY HISTORIC CHARLESTON FOUNDATION.

WATCHING THE GRAND FINALE AT MIDDLETON

PLAYING A GEM HORN — 1500'S

Dock Street Theatre
1937

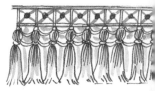

THE CURTAIN IS ALL DONE IN TROMPE L'OEIL.

THE RESTROOM SIGN — LIKE A TINY CHANDELIER

A CELL PHONE RINGS IN THE AUDIENCE. EVERYONE FROWNS & THERE IS A SCOLDING MURMUR. THEN A GIRL HANDS THE PHONE TO THE SOLOIST, AND SHE LAUNCHES INTO —

The Telephone
— AN OPERA BY GIAN CARLO MENOTTI (THE FATHER OF SPOLETO)

E ARLY CHARLESTONIANS LOVED THE ARTS AND HAD "GREAT DEMONSTRATIONS OF PLEASURE" — PARADES, MUSIC, AND THE FIRST PLAY ON THIS SITE IN 1736. ANTEBELLUM SPOLETO!

Spoleto Chamber music at Dock Street Theatre

HIS LEGS WERE ALWAYS MOVING.

HIS HAIR BOUNCES WHEN HE PLAYS RAVEL.

CHARLES WADSWORTH

ARTISTIC DIRECTOR FOR CHAMBER MUSIC. HAS BEEN WITH SPOLETO FROM ITS BIRTH HERE IN 1976.

39

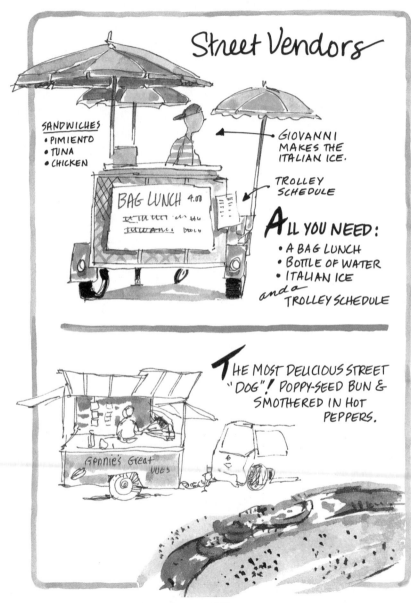

Street Vendors

SANDWICHES
- PIMIENTO
- TUNA
- CHICKEN

BAG LUNCH 4.00

GIOVANNI MAKES THE ITALIAN ICE.

TROLLEY SCHEDULE

ALL YOU NEED:
- A BAG LUNCH
- BOTTLE OF WATER
- ITALIAN ICE

and a TROLLEY SCHEDULE

THE MOST DELICIOUS STREET "DOG"! POPPY-SEED BUN & SMOTHERED IN HOT PEPPERS.

Gonnie's Great Dogs

ST. PHILIP'S EPISCOPAL CHURCH
1835

LILY OF THE VALLEY

THE GRAVE OF OUR LITTLE LILLIE

FOR THE FIRST SETTLERS, THIS WAS THE CHURCH OF CHARLESTON. THOSE NOT OF THE ANGLICAN FAITH WERE "DISSENTERS."

MANY FAMOUS PEOPLE ARE BURIED HERE AND ACROSS THE STREET IN THE "STRANGERS CHURCHYARD." EVEN IN DEATH, JOHN C. CALHOUN KEPT FALLING IN AND OUT OF FAVOR AND WAS MOVED BACK AND FORTH ACROSS THE STREET.

RESTAURANT

THE STORY GOES THAT WHEN MAJOR RHETT WAS ENTERTAINING PRESIDENT TAFT, RHETT'S BUTLER (GET IT?) THOUGHT THE CRAB SOUP WAS TOO THIN & ADDED BLUE CRAB ROE & SHERRY FOR THICKNESS.

AWARD-WINNING SHE-CRAB SOUP

ROUX: 1/4 lb. butter
      1/4 lb. flour

PREPARATION:
Melt butter and stir in flour to make roux. Add milk and cream and bring to boil. Add remaining ingredients. Simmer for 20 minutes. Garnish with sherried whipped cream.

INGREDIENTS:
1 cup heavy cream
3 cups milk
2 cups fish stock or water and fish base
1/4 lb. crab roe
1 lb. white crabmeat

1 cup chopped celery, lightly sautéed with:
1/4 cup chopped carrots
1/4 cup chopped onion
1/4 cup sherry wine
1 tbsp. Tabasco sauce
1 tbsp. Worcestershire sauce

Makes 12 servings.

Bags & Bonnets

SILK GARDENIAS

"Southern Lady"

"Charleston Window Box"

FAB BAGS BY "MOO ROO" MADE ON KING STREET.

"Bouquet of Roses"

ORIGINAL TIE STYLE

THE CHARLESTON BONNET

A COLONIAL TRADITION KEPT ALIVE BY THE STORE EIGHTY-TWO CHURCH. THEY ARE STILL MADE BY HAND WITH ROLLED & WHIPPED EDGING.

COSTUME CHAPEAUX FROM "MISS NICKI'S OLDE TIME PHOTOS."

The Carriage Trade

ENTERTAINING WAY TO SEE CHARLESTON —

AT PALMETTO CARRIAGE WORKS

WEDDING CARRIAGE

"LEVI" — FRENCH PERCHERON HORSE SOAKING A SORE ANKLE IN EPSOM SALTS AT OLDE TOWNE CARRIAGE COMPANY.

MULE — MALE DONKEY + FEMALE HORSE
JOHN — MALE MULE
MOLLY — FEMALE MULE
HINNY — MALE HORSE + FEMALE DONKEY
JENNY — FEMALE DONKEY

MULES & HINNIES — USUALLY STERILE

DON'T FEED FINGERS TO THE MULES

"FOR THE SPECIAL NEEDS OF OLDER HORSES"

EQUINE SENIOR

"Lottery"

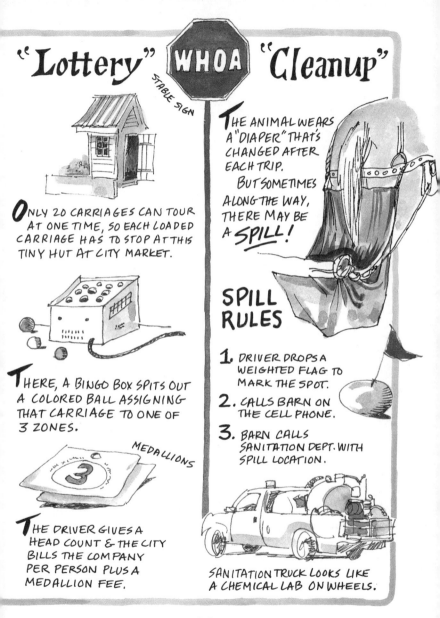

WHOA *STABLE SIGN*

"Cleanup"

ONLY 20 CARRIAGES CAN TOUR AT ONE TIME, SO EACH LOADED CARRIAGE HAS TO STOP AT THIS TINY HUT AT CITY MARKET.

THERE, A BINGO BOX SPITS OUT A COLORED BALL ASSIGNING THAT CARRIAGE TO ONE OF 3 ZONES.

MEDALLIONS

THE DRIVER GIVES A HEAD COUNT & THE CITY BILLS THE COMPANY PER PERSON PLUS A MEDALLION FEE.

THE ANIMAL WEARS A "DIAPER" THAT'S CHANGED AFTER EACH TRIP.

BUT SOMETIMES ALONG THE WAY, THERE MAY BE A *SPILL!*

SPILL RULES

1. DRIVER DROPS A WEIGHTED FLAG TO MARK THE SPOT.

2. CALLS BARN ON THE CELL PHONE.

3. BARN CALLS SANITATION DEPT. WITH SPILL LOCATION.

SANITATION TRUCK LOOKS LIKE A CHEMICAL LAB ON WHEELS.

OLD SLAVE MART MUSEUM

SKILLED SLAVES WERE FREQUENTLY HIRED OUT, BUT THE CITY GREW CONCERNED OVER SLAVES MOVING ABOUT FROM JOB TO JOB. PLUS OFFICIALS SAW A CHANCE TO COLLECT FEES.

SO BEGINNING IN 1818, OWNERS WERE REQUIRED TO ANNUALLY REGISTER SLAVES FOR HIRE.

SLAVES HAD TO WEAR THIS "BADGE"—WHAT IS NOW A COLLECTIBLE SLAVE TAG—MADE OF COPPER AND STAMPED WITH THEIR SKILLS.

COLLECTORS OFTEN SEARCH OLD PRIVIES FOR THESE TAGS.

CHARLESTON
264
PORTER
1842

POWERFUL REMINDERS OF SLAVERY

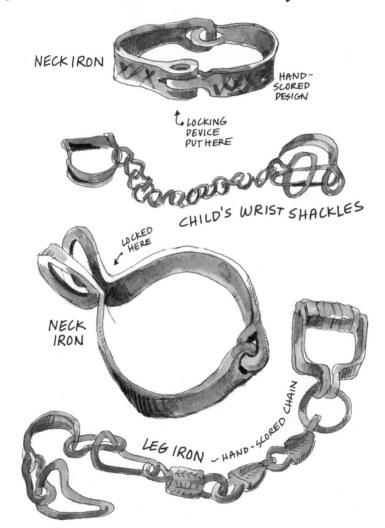

NECK IRON

HAND-SCORED DESIGN

↳ LOCKING DEVICE PUT HERE

CHILD'S WRIST SHACKLES

LOCKED HERE ←

NECK IRON

LEG IRON – HAND-SCORED CHAIN

Waterfront Park

VENDUE FOUNTAIN

KIDS LOVE PLAYING IN THIS CIRCULAR SPRAY FOUNTAIN. THEY SHOW UP IN THEIR BATHING SUITS AND GOGGLES!

PINEAPPLE FOUNTAIN

BEAUTIFULLY DESIGNED AND A SYMBOL OF CHARLESTON'S HOSPITALITY

DETAIL

The Jenkins Orphanage Band

REVEREND DANIEL JENKINS FOUND 4 YOUNG WAIFS HUDDLED BEHIND A WOODPILE IN 1892 & DECIDED TO START AN ORPHANAGE FOR BLACK CHILDREN.

MONEY WAS SCARCE, SO HE ASKED CITIZENS FOR USED INSTRUMENTS, HIRED MUSIC TEACHERS, AND CREATED A LITTLE BAND.

THE "CONDUCTOR" ALSO DID SOMERSAULTS & DANCED.

THE ORPHANS PLAYED RAGTIME & JAZZ ON CHARLESTON STREET CORNERS FOR MONEY AND DID A "CRAZY GEECHIE DANCE."

LOCAL TOUR GUIDE LORE: THIS WAS THE ORIGIN OF

The Charleston

THE GIG WAS SO SUCCESSFUL THEY TOOK IT ON THE ROAD TO NEW YORK AND ENGLAND, WHERE THEY WERE FINED FOR STOPPING TRAFFIC.

1930's

THE BAND TRAVELED IN OLD CITADEL UNIFORMS.

SLIGHTLY NORTH OF BROAD
(S.N.O.B.)

FACING THIS KITCHEN IS A LONG, LOW BAR CALLED THE "CHEF'S TABLE" FOR SPECIAL TASTINGS & SINGLE DINERS. THERE ARE EVEN MAGAZINES TO READ.

TOMATOES

Magnolias Uptown Down South

CRAB & ARTICHOKE TOPPING

SAUTÉED GROUPER

HERB POTATO CAKE

Hominy & Grits

CHARLESTON
BREAKFAST:
SHRIMP & GRITS
& TASSO SAUCE

HOMINY– NATIVE AMERICANS WERE THE FIRST TO GRIND UP CORN INTO COARSE GRAINS THEY CALLED **"TOCKAHOMINIE"**

GRITS (GRIST)– WHAT SOUTHERNERS CALLED GRISTMILL GROUND, UNCOOKED CORN. WHEN COOKED IT WAS – **HOMINY.**

TODAY, THE TERMS HOMINY & GRITS ARE INTERCHANGEABLE.

LITTLE-KNOWN FACT– GRITS START AS WHOLE WHITE CORN KERNELS SOAKED IN LYE WATER! THEN THEY'RE DRIED AND PREFERABLY "STONE" GROUND TO A COARSE TEXTURE.

GRITS AT THE HOMINY GRILL

TODAY'S BIRDS:
PIGEONS

OLD CITY MARKET

FIRST A MEAT MARKET, IT HAS
ALWAYS BUSTLED WITH
VENDORS & SHOPPERS.

FLOWER
VENDOR
1900

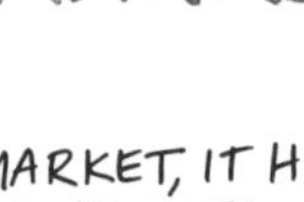

FISHMONGER
1959

"CHARLESTON EAGLE"

BUZZARDS ONCE TROLLED
THE MARKET FOR MEAT
SCRAPS. THEY KEPT THE
PLACE CLEAN & WERE
PROTECTED BY LAW.

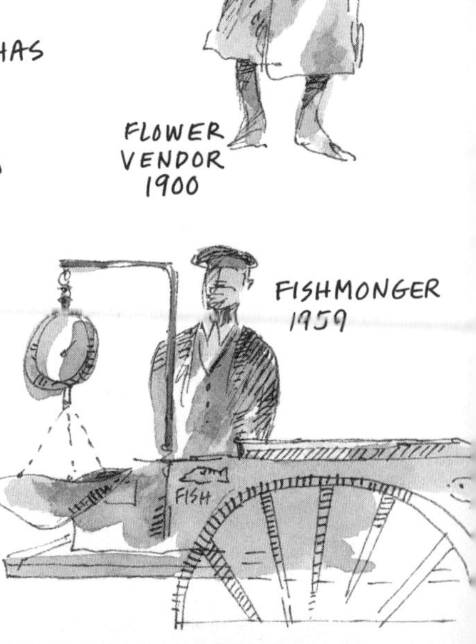

FISH

KAHAL KADOSH BETH ELOHIM
SYNAGOGUE
1840

SEPHARDIC ORTHODOX JEWS CAME HERE AS EARLY AS 1695.

IN REBUILDING AFTER THE FIRE OF 1838, SOME WANTED TO MODERNIZE THE RITUALS PLUS HAVE AN ORGAN, SINCE INSTRUMENTS HADN'T BEEN ALLOWED.

ORTHODOX JEWS REFUSED AND THE DEBATE LANDED IN COURT.

CHANTING

TANAKH

THE REFORMERS WON AND THIS BECAME THE:

FIRST REFORM JEWISH CONGREGATION IN AMERICA.

OLDEST SYNAGOGUE IN CONTINUOUS USE IN AMERICA.

SECOND-OLDEST SYNAGOGUE IN AMERICA.

53

CENTRAL STATION 1887
CHARLESTON FIRE DEPARTMENT

ORIGINALLY BUILT FOR HORSE-DRAWN ENGINES, TODAY'S ENGINE IS CUSTOM-MADE TO FIT THE SMALL OPENING.

GROOVES TO GIVE HORSES TRACTION

CHARLESTON WAS THE 2ND TOWN IN AMERICA TO HAVE A "WATER ENGINE" AND THEY STILL HAVE IT! THE STATION IS NOT KNOWN AS A MUSEUM, BUT SNEAK A PEEK AT THEIR ENGINE COLLECTION.

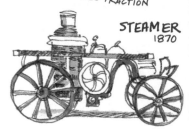

STEAMER 1870

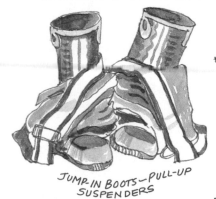

JUMP-IN BOOTS—PULL-UP SUSPENDERS

"WATER ENGINE" FROM ENGLAND, 1760

54

Charleston "Firsts"

CHARLESTON WAS THE FIRST CITY IN AMERICA TO HAVE A:

- CHAMBER OF COMMERCE, 1773

- THEATER (DOCK STREET THEATRE), 1736

- FIRE INSURANCE COMPANY, 1736

- WOMAN NEWSPAPER EDITOR & PUBLISHER (MRS. ELIZABETH TIMOTHY), 1739

- FORMAL LANDSCAPE GARDEN (MIDDLETON PLACE), 1741

- PUBLIC LIBRARY, 1743

- MUSEUM, 1773

- PRESCRIPTION DRUG STORE, 1780

- MUNICIPAL COLLEGE (THE COLLEGE OF CHARLESTON), 1770

- AGRICULTURAL SOCIETY, 1785

- REFORM JEWISH CONGREGATION, 1844

- PASSENGER TRAIN SERVICE (TO HAMBURG S.C.), 1830

- FIRST SHOT OF THE CIVIL WAR, 1861

- SUCCESSFUL SUBMARINE ATTACK (THE HUNLEY SANK THE WARSHIP HOUSATONIC), 1864

- HISTORIC PRESERVATION SOCIETY, 1931

WOOD NYMPH IN MIDDLETON GARDEN

AT THE JOSEPH MANIGAULT HOUSE

Philip Simmons

*T*HIS MASTER BLACKSMITH BEGAN WORKING IN 1925 AS AN APPRENTICE TO A FORMER SLAVE. HE LEARNED THE CRAFT OF DECORATIVE WROUGHT-IRON WORK AND CREATED MANY FAMOUS GATES OVER HIS LIFETIME. HE'S KNOWN AS "THE KEEPER OF THE GATE."

FAVORITE 100-YR-OLD HAMMER

LIKES TO TAKE PHOTOS WITH IT.

DRAWN IN HIS CHURCH CLOTHES

EVEN THE SMITHSONIAN HAS A SIMMONS GATE! AT THEIR INVITATION, HE SET UP HIS FORGE AT THE ANNUAL AMERICAN FOLKLIFE FESTIVAL IN WASHINGTON, D.C.

opening

PILLAR.

55"

36

gate 50

PLANS FOR A GATE HE & APPRENTICES CRAFTED AT THE D.C. FESTIVAL

THE PHILIP SIMMONS GARDEN

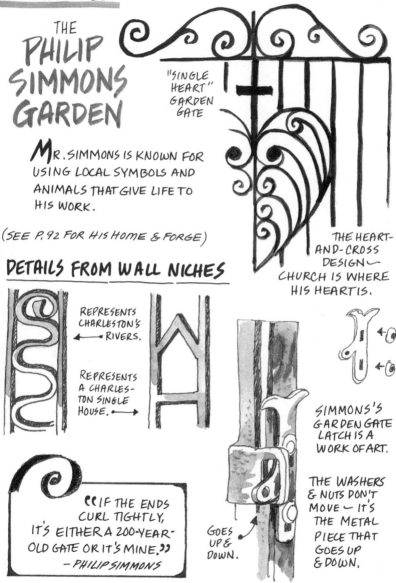

"SINGLE HEART" GARDEN GATE

MR. SIMMONS IS KNOWN FOR USING LOCAL SYMBOLS AND ANIMALS THAT GIVE LIFE TO HIS WORK.

(SEE P.92 FOR HIS HOME & FORGE)

THE HEART-AND-CROSS DESIGN— CHURCH IS WHERE HIS HEART IS.

DETAILS FROM WALL NICHES

REPRESENTS CHARLESTON'S ←→ RIVERS.

REPRESENTS A CHARLESTON SINGLE HOUSE. →

SIMMONS'S GARDEN GATE LATCH IS A WORK OF ART.

THE WASHERS & NUTS DON'T MOVE — IT'S THE METAL PIECE THAT GOES UP & DOWN.

GOES UP & DOWN.

"IF THE ENDS CURL TIGHTLY, IT'S EITHER A 200-YEAR-OLD GATE OR IT'S MINE."
— PHILIP SIMMONS

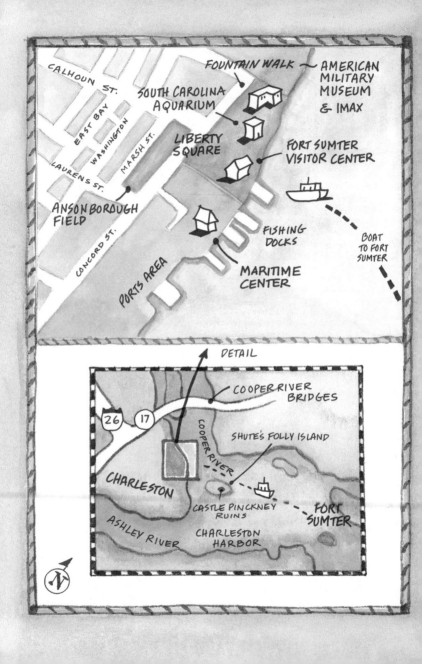

THE ORIGINAL COOPER RIVER BRIDGES

CHAPTER 3
CHARLESTON HARBOR

THE ASHLEY AND COOPER RIVERS THAT FLOW INTO CHARLESTON HARBOR WERE NAMED AFTER LORD ANTHONY ASHLEY COOPER, ONE OF EIGHT LORDS PROPRIETORS WHO FINANCED THE COLONY AND ESTABLISHED THE HARBOR AS A THRIVING SHIPPING PORT.

THE JOHN P. GRACE MEMORIAL & THE SILAS N. PEARMAN BRIDGES SPANNING THE COOPER RIVER ARE LOVELY TO LOOK AT BUT CANNOT HANDLE THE TRAFFIC. THEY ARE BEING REPLACED BY A MODERN SPAN BRIDGE.

CELEBRATING FLAG DAY   AT THE FORT SUMTER FACILITY

Ports Area

CHARLESTON IS THE 7th LARGEST CONTAINER PORT IN THE U.S. & THE ACTIVITY IS FASCINATING TO WATCH.

THE FAÇADE OF THE BENNETT RICE MILL

THOUSANDS OF CARS SHIPPED ALMOST DAILY —

(ANY HISTORICAL BUILDING WORTH ITS SALT HAS A PALMETTO TREE — A CHARLESTON SYMBOL.)

TUGBOATS SWING HUGE CONTAINER SHIPS 180° & GUIDE THEM TO A BERTH.

EACH SHIP IN THIS LINE IS NAMED AFTER AN OPERA.

BOHEME

TUG

MARKINGS ON THE BOW TELL THE TUG-BOAT CAPTAIN WHERE TO PUSH.

Maritime Center

WOODEN BOAT APPRECIATION DAY & FAMILY BOATBUILDING

THE REIDS FAMILY

LOTS OF JOBS FOR KIDS

*E*ACH YEAR, TEAMS OF FAMILIES AND FRIENDS SPEND THE WEEKEND UNDER A TENT, BUILDING A CHARLESTON BATEAU. TEAMS GET A KIT OF MAHOGANY MARINE PLYWOOD AND SPANISH CEDAR PARTS. ON SUNDAY, THE UNPAINTED SKIFFS ARE CAULKED & LAUNCHED.

20-YEAR-OLD HOMEMADE TOOLBOX

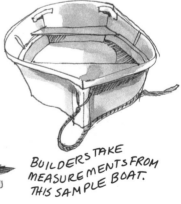

BUILDERS TAKE MEASUREMENTS FROM THIS SAMPLE BOAT.

COOPER RIVER TRAFFIC

THE YORKTOWN

REGATTA NIGHT—
EVERY
WEDNESDAY

A LITTLE PARTY FERRY

OCEANGOING FREIGHTERS

EVENING SCHOONER TOUR

TUG LOOKS
LIKE A
DR. SEUSS
CREATION!

Gone Fishin'

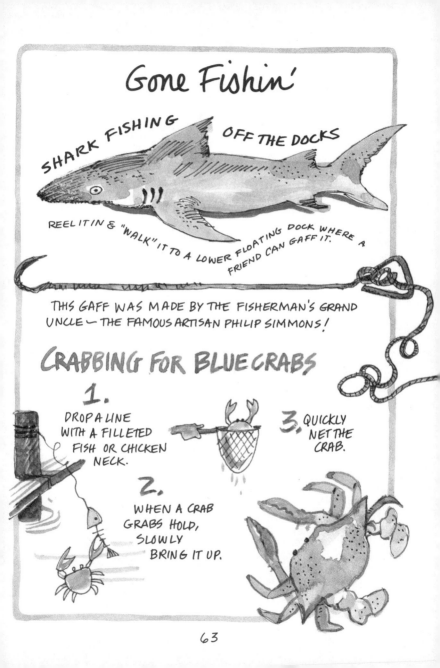

SHARK FISHING OFF THE DOCKS

REEL IT IN & "WALK" IT TO A LOWER FLOATING DOCK WHERE A FRIEND CAN GAFF IT.

THIS GAFF WAS MADE BY THE FISHERMAN'S GRAND UNCLE — THE FAMOUS ARTISAN PHILIP SIMMONS!

CRABBING FOR BLUE CRABS

1. DROP A LINE WITH A FILLETED FISH OR CHICKEN NECK.

2. WHEN A CRAB GRABS HOLD, SLOWLY BRING IT UP.

3. QUICKLY NET THE CRAB.

FORT SUMTER

CASTLE PINCKNEY

Fort Sumter VISITOR EDUCATION & TOUR BOAT FACILITY

*T*OUR BOATS TRAVEL FROM HERE OUT TO FORT SUMTER, NAMED AFTER THOMAS SUMTER, A SOUTH CAROLINA REVOLUTIONARY WAR PATRIOT.

THE CIVIL WAR STARTED HERE
APRIL 12, 1861

- AFTER SOUTH CAROLINA SECEDED, MAJ. ANDERSON AND HIS UNION TROOPS MOVED FROM FORT MOULTRIE TO FORT SUMTER.
- THE SOUTH TOLD THEM TO EVACUATE OR ELSE!
- ANDERSON STAYED AND GEN. BEAUREGARD BEGAN FIRING.
- AFTER 34 HOURS, ANDERSON SURRENDERED & NO ONE WAS KILLED.

HURRICANE HUGO DESTROYED THIS CANNON'S ORIGINAL CARRIAGE.

BLOCKS WILL BE REPLACED BY A REPRODUCTION CARRIAGE.

CANNON HAS A RANGE OF 3803 YARDS.

SUMTER GUARD C. 1880

The Flags of Sumter

*T*HESE FLAGS WERE AT SUMTER AT VARIOUS TIMES DURING THE CIVIL WAR.

1859

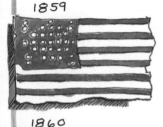

UNION FLAG

ARRANGEMENT OF THE 33 STARS WAS ARBITRARY. THIS IS THE ORIGINAL FLAG THAT FLEW HERE AT THE START OF THE CIVIL WAR AND CAME DOWN 2 DAYS LATER.

1860

PALMETTO GUARD FLAG

THE PALMETTO GUARD WAS THE 1ST CONFEDERATE INFANTRY TO ENTER FORT SUMTER AND PLACE THIS FLAG ON THE WALL.

1863

1861

"STARS & BARS"

1ST CONFEDERATE FLAG REPLACED THE UNION FLAG — 7 STARS FOR SECEDED STATES.

"STAINLESS BANNER"

2ND CONFEDERATE FLAG — SCRAPPED BECAUSE WHEN LIMP, IT LOOKED LIKE A SURRENDER FLAG.

Civil War Fashion

THE SEWING MACHINE WAS INVENTED ABOUT 10 YEARS BEFORE THE CIVIL WAR. TODAY'S "RE-CREATORS" ARE ABLE TO USE IT TO MAKE THE HISTORICALLY ACCURATE FASHIONS THEY WEAR.

PINS STUCK IN A CLOTH

JEAN SEWS ON THIS 1906 SINGER.

← A "SHOW YOUR CHARMS" NECKLINE

BACK

Ball Gown — THERE WERE NO HEM PROTECTORS ON THE FINER GOWNS SO LADIES BROUGHT THEIR DRESSES TO THE PARTY & CHANGED.

GUESTS STAYED OVERNIGHT, & NEXT DAY WORE THE SAME GOWN WITH A ...

Second-Day Bodice

BASE OF HAT RESTS ON THE BUN.

← JET BUTTONS

CURTAIN →

JEAN, A "LIVING HISTORIAN"

IN THE FRONT, NO BUTTONHOLES USED — HOOKS & EYES.

BONNET STRINGS

DROP SHOULDER WITH PIPING FOR STRENGTH, SUPPORT, & VISUAL INTEREST.

TRIPLE PAGODA SLEEVES

REMOVABLE UNDERSLEEVES FOR WASHING

SKIRT TAKES 5-9 YARDS OF MATERIAL TO GO OVER HOOP.

HOOPS, PETTICOATS, & TOP SKIRT WEIGHED ABOUT 40 lbs. — LADIES FREQUENTLY FAINTED!

4-8" HEM ADDS WEIGHT.

HEM PROTECTER

COTTON EDGING IS PART OF A LARGE HEM. AS IT BECOMES DIRTY, THE HEM IS TURNED.

A "LATE WAR" WORK DRESS. AS THE WAR DRAGGED ON, FABRIC BECAME SCARCE — SO DRESSES WERE PATCHED & FABRIC WAS HOMESPUN.

NO HOOP

SOUTH CAROLINA
Aquarium

THE FOCUS OF THIS UNIQUE NONPROFIT INSTITUTION IS TO EDUCATE THE PUBLIC ABOUT THE DIVERSE AREAS OF SOUTH CAROLINA WILDLIFE AND CONSERVATION THROUGH ITS EXHIBITS.

The Mountain Forest

PLAYFUL OTTERS FROM THE COLD, RUSHING RIVERS OF THE BLUE RIDGE MOUNTAINS.

The Piedmont

THE PLATEAU AT THE BASE OF THE BLUE RIDGE MOUNTAINS — WITH ROLLING HILLS, VALLEYS, & STREAMS.

YELLOW-BELLIED TURTLE

The Coastal Plain

A LOW-LYING REGION CLOSE TO THE OCEAN — INCLUDES SWAMPS.

WEBBED!

BABY AMERICAN ALLIGATOR

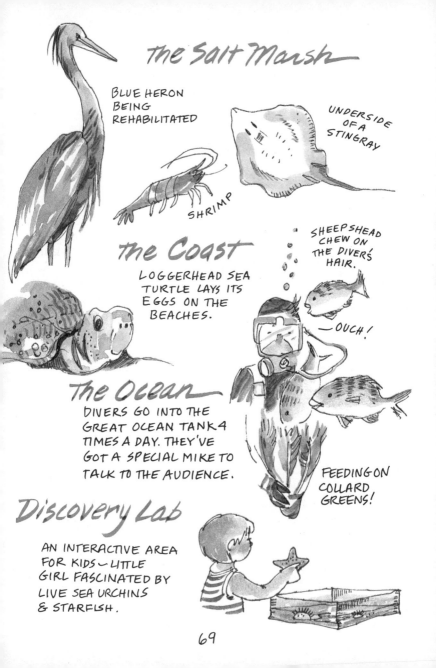

The Salt Marsh

BLUE HERON BEING REHABILITATED

UNDERSIDE OF A STINGRAY

SHRIMP

The Coast

LOGGERHEAD SEA TURTLE LAYS ITS EGGS ON THE BEACHES.

SHEEPSHEAD CHEW ON THE DIVER'S HAIR.

—OUCH!

The Ocean

DIVERS GO INTO THE GREAT OCEAN TANK 4 TIMES A DAY. THEY'VE GOT A SPECIAL MIKE TO TALK TO THE AUDIENCE.

FEEDING ON COLLARD GREENS!

Discovery Lab

AN INTERACTIVE AREA FOR KIDS — LITTLE GIRL FASCINATED BY LIVE SEA URCHINS & STARFISH.

69

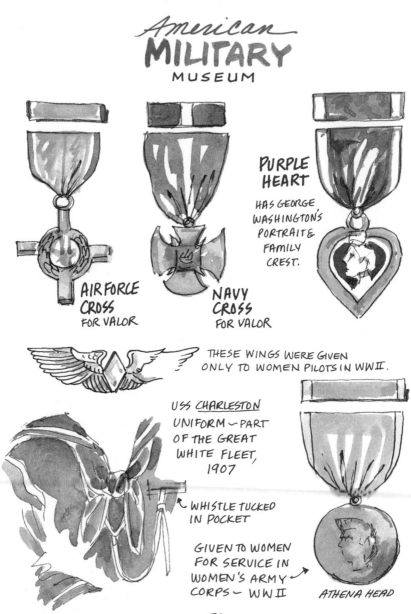

American
MILITARY
MUSEUM

PURPLE HEART

HAS GEORGE WASHINGTON'S PORTRAIT & FAMILY CREST.

AIR FORCE CROSS FOR VALOR

NAVY CROSS FOR VALOR

THESE WINGS WERE GIVEN ONLY TO WOMEN PILOTS IN WWII.

USS CHARLESTON UNIFORM — PART OF THE GREAT WHITE FLEET, 1907

WHISTLE TUCKED IN POCKET

GIVEN TO WOMEN FOR SERVICE IN WOMEN'S ARMY CORPS — WWII

ATHENA HEAD

70

Spirit of South Carolina

A PILOT SCHOONER

CHARLESTON IS THE HOME PORT
FOR THE NEW TALL SHIP
SPIRIT OF SOUTH CAROLINA,
BUILT IN ANSONBOROUGH
FIELD IN 2002.

- TRAINING VESSEL
  FOR YOUNG SAILORS
- FLOATING MUSEUM
- MODIFIED TO
  MEET COAST
  GUARD
  STANDARDS
- 140' LONG, 10.5' DRAFT

- "LINES"
  TAKEN FROM
  PLANS FOUND AT
  THE SMITHSONIAN

- THE ORIGINAL WAS BUILT IN
  1879 AT PREGNALL BROTHERS
  SHIPYARD, CHARLESTON.

Laying of the Keel

FROM SURINAM—
ROT RESISTANT

THE PROJECT BEGAN BY LAYING
TWO 45' LONG ANGELIQUE
HARDWOOD TIMBERS END TO
END. WHEN JOINED, THEY BE-
CAME THE BACKBONE OF THE
SHIP, RUNNING FROM STEM
TO STERN.

71

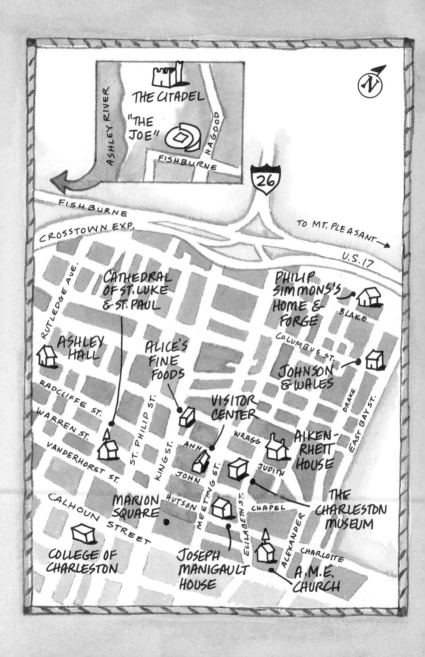

CATCH A TROLLEY AT THE VISITOR CENTER AND GO ALL OVER TOWN!

CHAPTER 4

NORTH OF CALHOUN

These were the suburbs when the Manigault and Aiken homes were built here in the early 1800's.

Today, this part of Charleston is changing and growing with museums and businesses blending easily with old neighborhoods.

Up here are wonderful places like Miss Alice's Soul Food Restaurant, the swinging "Mother Emanuel" Church, the bustling Visitor Center, a festive Farmers Market, and the joyful, carnival atmosphere of Baseball games at "The Joe."

SAILOR'S HAT FROM THE USS *CHARLESTON*

USS CHARLES

73

"Mother Emanuel"

EMANUEL AFRICAN METHODIST EPISCOPAL CHURCH
1891

ALL THE LADIES IN HATS WENT UP TO THE ALTAR & KNEELED.

VESEY MEMORIAL AT A.M.E.

CHURCH MEMBER & SLAVE DENMARK VESEY PLAYED THE LOTTERY AND WON HIS FREEDOM. BUT IN 1822, HIS ELABORATE INSURRECTION PLOT AGAINST WHITES WAS FOILED. HE & 34 OTHERS WERE HUNG. TODAY, HE'S REMEMBERED AS A POLITICAL & SPIRITUAL LEADER OF THE A.M.E. CHURCH.

If you must whisper, whisper a prayer— If you must talk, talk to God.

REVEREND SMITH

Amen

CLAP
CLAP

CLAP
CLAP

THE CHURCH <u>ROCKS</u>!
SINGING, CLAPPING,
PIANO, & DRUMS.

USHERETTES — IN WHITE
UNIFORMS, COTTON GLOVES, & A
HANKIE "CORSAGE"

USHER

ONE HAND BEHIND
THE BACK— THE
USHERETTE POSE

75

Porgy and Bess

A PICCOLO SPOLETO FESTIVAL EVENT HELD AT THE EMANUEL A.M.E. CHURCH.

THE CHORALIERS MUSIC CLUB SANG EXCERPTS FROM GEORGE GERSHWIN'S FOLK OPERA BASED ON THE BOOK _PORGY_ BY CHARLESTON POET DUBOSE HEYWARD. IT DEPICTS "THE NEGRO LIFE OF THE CITY" & THE FURY OF THE 1911 HURRICANE.

CABBAGE ROW ON CHURCH STREET DOWNTOWN WAS A TENEMENT COURTYARD WHERE VEGETABLES WERE SOLD. THIS WAS HEYWARD'S INSPIRATION FOR THE FICTIONAL "CATFISH ROW" HE SET ON EAST BAY STREET DOWNTOWN.

77

MARION SQUARE

JAZZ ON THE GREEN

CHARLESTON
FARMERS MARKET

"Lettuce Entertain You"

AND THEY DO! EVERY SUMMER
SATURDAY
LOWCOUNTRY PRODUCE, FLOWERS, ARTISTS, CRAFTS, FOOD, GARDEN GURUS, VISITING CHEFS, RECY- CLING IDEAS, MUSICIANS, SHOWS FOR KIDS.

THE BEST COLLARD GREENS BECAUSE THEY'RE GROWN IN GOOD SOUTH CAROLINA SANDY SOIL.

HAND SHELLED BUTTER BEANS

Zinnias
$3.50/bunch

PEACHES & EGGPLANT FROM JOHN'S ISLAND — ZINNIAS FROM A HOME GARDEN

PUMPKIN CHIPS

AN OLD PLANTATION RECIPE — PRESERVED

BREAD FROM A FRENCH BAKERY IN TOWN

Alice's

FINE FOODS & SOUTHERN COOKING

MISS ALICE

SOUL FOOD EVERY DAY & JAZZ ON SUNDAYS— LIFE DOESN'T GET MUCH BETTER THAN THAT!

ALICE'S ICE TEA NOW SOLD BY THE GALLON

LIVER & GIZZARD 4.2.25 PER ORDER

REGGIE

THE SINGING WAITER WHO KEEPS THE ICE TEA & LEMONADE ACOMIN'.

Gullah

"Latah"
(LATER)

AFRICAN SLAVES IN THE LOWCOUNTRY CREATED A LANGUAGE AND CULTURE THEY CALLED GULLAH. THE WORD MAY HAVE COME FROM THE GOLA OR GORA TRIBES IN ANGOLA.

ALPHONSO BROWN GIVES GULLAH TOURS.

RED AND "HAINT BLUE" PAINT KEEP THE SPIRITS OUT.

THE GULLAH LANGUAGE, MADE OFFICIAL IN 1939, IS A CREOLE-BASED LANGUAGE WITH ENGLISH AS ITS MAIN BASE.

CHAA'STON = CHARLESTON
HAINT = GHOST/SPIRIT
BUBBA = MALE NAME
AXS ME = ASK ME
GOOBER = PEANUT
TOTE = CARRY

DAUGHTERS OF THE SOUTH

COPY OF A DETAIL FROM A PAINTING BY JONATHAN GREEN

The Schools of Charleston

THE CITADEL 1842

A FORTRESS (NOW A HOTEL ON MEETING STREET) WHERE CADETS GUARDED THE STATE ARSENAL AND TRAINED AS LEADERS AT "THE MILITARY COLLEGE OF SOUTH CAROLINA". THE CITADEL RELOCATED ALONG THE ASHLEY RIVER IN 1922.

1895 RING

1989 RING   *PUT ABOARD THE SPACE SHUTTLE COLUMBIA IN 1989.*

IN THE MUSEUM—A CADET ROOM CLOTHES PRESS, 1906

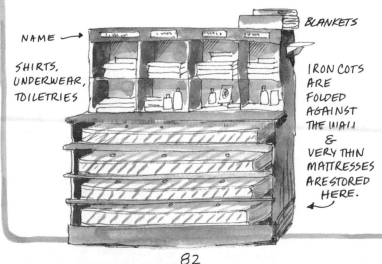

NAME →

BLANKETS

SHIRTS, UNDERWEAR, TOILETRIES

IRON COTS ARE FOLDED AGAINST THE WALL & VERY THIN MATTRESSES ARE STORED HERE.

82

YOU CAN
TELL IT'S
A SMALL
SCHOOL
BY THE
SIZE OF
THE BUS!

ASHLEY HALL 1909

*F*OUNDER MISS MARY VARDRINE McBEE WANTED A
SCHOOL WHERE FAMILIES COULD "CONFIDE THEIR TENDER
BLOSSOMS TO HER CARE." TODAY, THE SCHOOL OFFERS
GIRLS A SOLID EDUCATION IN THE LIBERAL ARTS
AND SCIENCES.

THE "SHELL HOUSE" ON CAMPUS IS A
HANGOUT FOR SENIORS ONLY.

OUTSIDE IS
COVERED IN
CONCH SHELLS.

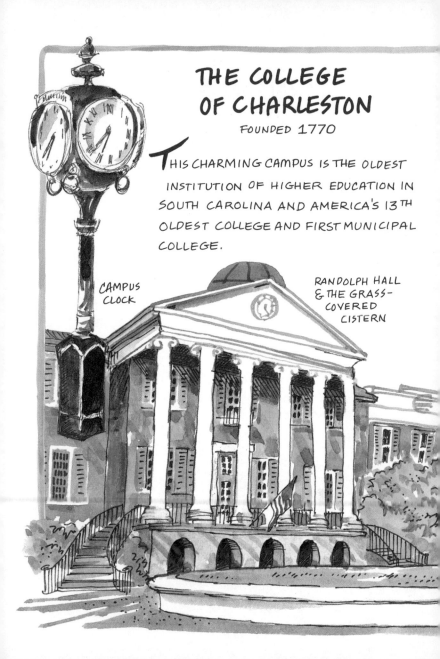

THE COLLEGE OF CHARLESTON

FOUNDED 1770

THIS CHARMING CAMPUS IS THE OLDEST INSTITUTION OF HIGHER EDUCATION IN SOUTH CAROLINA AND AMERICA'S 13TH OLDEST COLLEGE AND FIRST MUNICIPAL COLLEGE.

CAMPUS CLOCK

RANDOLPH HALL & THE GRASS-COVERED CISTERN

JOHNSON & WALES
UNIVERSITY 1984

*A*N INTERNATIONALLY RESPECTED
CULINARY AND HOSPITALITY SCHOOL
CALLED "AMERICA'S CAREER
UNIVERSITY."

CLASSROOM SIGN

220 STOCKS & SAUCES

NECKERCHIEFS:
INSTRUCTOR

WALL TILE MATCHES PANTS.

CULINARY ARTS

BAKERY/PASTRY

4 SCHOOL DAYS A WEEK

HOSPITALITY

3 TRI-MESTERS

SLEEVE POCKET

THE "STEP & FLAME" J&W LOGO IN RE-VERSE IS THE CHECKERED PANTS FABRIC.

85

Cathedral of St. Luke and St. Paul
1815

As part of the Spoleto Festival, the Westminster Choir sang the Lord's Prayer in English, Latin, & French.

LORD'S PRAYER SET IN ALCOVE

Our Father

THE CHARLESTON MUSEUM 1773

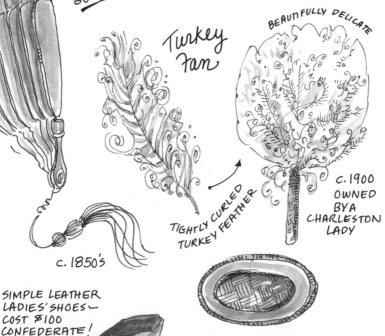

"PEEKING" MIRROR

THE END IS CALLED A GUARD.

BECAUSE IT'S AMERICA'S FIRST MUSEUM, THERE ARE COLLECTIONS FROM EARLY CHARLESTON FAMILIES, PLANTERS, PATRIOTS, AND SCIENTISTS.

Turkey Fan

BEAUTIFULLY DELICATE

TIGHTLY CURLED TURKEY FEATHER

c. 1900 OWNED BY A CHARLESTON LADY

c. 1850's

SIMPLE LEATHER LADIES' SHOES — COST $100 CONFEDERATE!

BROOCH MADE FROM A LOVED ONE'S HAIR. HAIR JEWELRY & ART WERE VERY POPULAR AS MEMENTOS IN THE 19TH CENTURY.

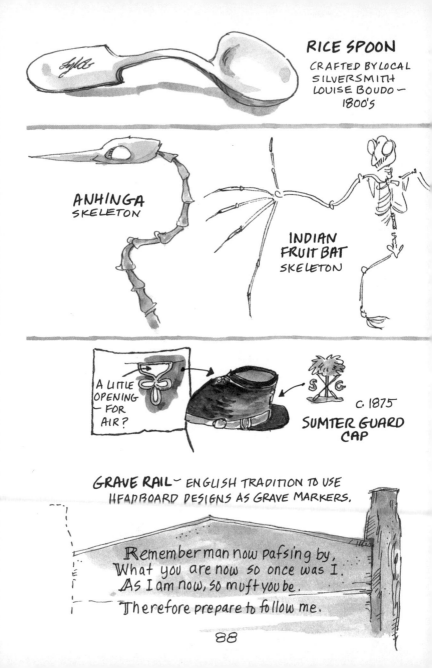

RICE SPOON

CRAFTED BY LOCAL
SILVERSMITH
LOUISE BOUDO —
1800'S

ANHINGA
SKELETON

INDIAN
FRUIT BAT
SKELETON

A LITTLE
OPENING
— FOR
AIR?

c. 1875

SUMTER GUARD
CAP

GRAVE RAIL — ENGLISH TRADITION TO USE
HEADBOARD DESIGNS AS GRAVE MARKERS.

Remember man now pafsing by,
What you are now so once was I.
As I am now, so muft you be.

Therefore prepare to follow me.

JOSEPH MANIGAULT HOUSE 1803

DESIGNED BY HIS BROTHER GABRIEL, A "GENTLEMAN-ARCHITECT," THIS ADAM-STYLE ARCHITECTURE WAS POPULAR AFTER THE REVOLUTIONARY WAR. THE ELEGANT SIMPLICITY WAS A CHANGE FROM THE RICH GEORGIAN DETAIL.

REAL DOOR →   ← FALSE DOOR FOR SYMMETRY

RICE BED — MAHOGANY BEDPOSTS CARVED WITH RICE PLANTS. MADE IN CHARLESTON.

WINTER BED   ## SUMMER BED

MOSQUITO NET REPLACED DRAPES.

HEADBOARD SLIDES OUT FOR AIR FLOW.

HEAVY DRAPES & BEDSPREAD

BED ROLLED AROUND THE ROOM TO CATCH THE AIR.

MANTLE PIECES

MANTLE CLOCK SEEMS TO BE THE SAME ONE IN A FAMILY PORTRAIT FROM THE 1700'S.

ON THE BEDROOM MANTLE

JIB DOORS IN THE BEDROOM ARE A FASHIONABLE GRAY.

NECESSITY CHAIR

CHARLESTONIANS CALLED BATHROOMS **"NECESSITIES."**

THIS TOILET LOOKS COMFORTABLE, LIKE A LIBRARY CHAIR WITH ARMS. WHEN THE LID IS DOWN, IT LOOKS LIKE A DRESSER.

AIKEN-RHETT HOUSE 1817

(A)

(B)

A UNIQUE TOWNHOUSE COMPLEX, WITH SLAVE QUARTERS, STABLES, AND PRIVIES THAT HAVE BEEN "CONSERVED RATHER THAN RESTORED."

PARTS OF THE HOUSE WERE SEALED FROM 1918 TO 1975, SO THERE ARE STILL ORIGINAL FURNISHINGS FROM GOV. AIKEN'S EUROPEAN SHOPPING TRIPS.

THE FADED WALLPAPERS ARE ALSO ORIGINAL, BUT WERE WATER DAMAGED IN 1989 BY HURRICANE HUGO.

(A) SLAVE "DORMS" OVER THE KITCHEN

(B) PRIVY IN THE CORNER OF THE PROPERTY

(C) AIKEN LIBRARY SELECTION

(C)

POWER OF SOLITUDE

THE LIFE OF BENJAMIN FRANKLIN & ILLUSTRATED

BRIGHT IDEAS FOR EVERYTHING

WAR OF THE REBELLION • OFFICIAL RECORDS OF THE UNION & CONFEDERATE ARMIES

THE RELIGIOUS OPINIONS & CHARACTER OF WASHINGTON

Philip Simmons's Home & Forge

A LIVING MUSEUM

FAMED BLACKSMITH PHILIP SIMMONS'S FORGE IS IN THE 1860 BUILDING BEHIND HIS HOME.

FIRE COLOR:

ORANGE — NOT READY

WHITE — READY

HOMEMADE FORGE

"The rhythm comes to you — can't teach that."

NEPHEW CARLTON SIMMONS

ANVIL
60 YRS. OLD

STUMP
ANCIENT DOGWOOD

WATERING CAN

SIMMONS MAKES MANY OF HIS OWN TOOLS, LIKE THIS TIN CAN WITH HOLES USED TO ADD WATER TO A TOO-HOT FIRE.

MAKING A SIGNATURE

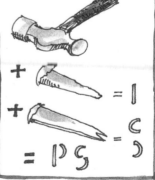

FISHBURNE STREET

FRIDAY NIGHT FIREWORKS AFTER THE GAME

"The Joe"

JOSEPH P. RILEY JR. PARK
1997

LADIES' NIGHT
FREE FOR ANYONE IN A SKIRT!

THE CITY'S FIRST BASEBALL TEAM WAS THE SEA GULLS (EST. 1886). NOW THEY'RE THE CHARLESTON RIVERDOGS, A CLASS A FARM TEAM FOR THE TAMPA BAY DEVIL RAYS. PART OWNER & DIRECTOR OF FUN IS ACTOR BILL MURRAY.

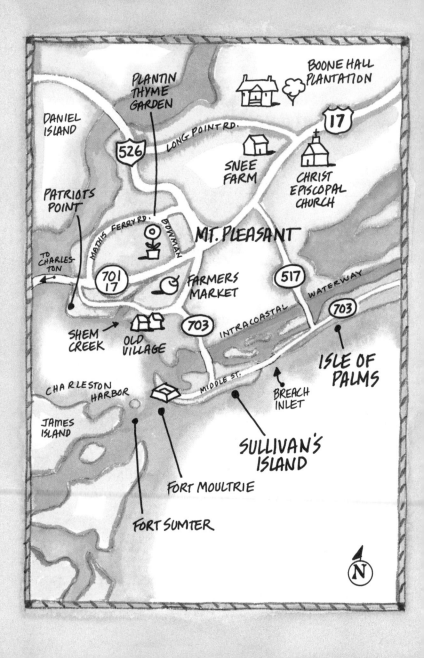

GNAT SHACK ON SHEM CREEK

CHAPTER 5

MT. PLEASANT &
THE ISLANDS

AS A PORT CITY, CHARLESTON PLAYED A SIGNIFICANT PART
IN BOTH THE REVOLUTIONARY WAR AND THE CIVIL WAR.

AT FORT MOULTRIE, PATRIOTS WON AN UNUSUAL BUT
IMPORTANT VICTORY AGAINST THE BRITISH DURING THE
"REV WAR."

THEN IN THE CIVIL WAR, THE HUNLEY, A SUBMARINE
BUILT BY THE SOUTH, SCORED A SURPRISE VICTORY
AGAINST THE HOUSATONIC, A UNION SHIP.

Hellooo

Hellooo

CANNON

A CALL TO ARMS?

95

PATRIOTS POINT
NAVAL & MARITIME MUSEUM

FLOATING & LAND-BASED EXHIBITS

USS YORKTOWN

BEFORE 1960, MANY AIRCRAFT CARRIERS WERE NAMED AFTER REVOLUTIONARY WAR EVENTS. (THE BRITISH SURRENDERED AT YORKTOWN, VA.)

ALSO KNOWN AS

"The Fighting Lady" 1943

THE FIRST YORKTOWN (CV-5) WAS LOST IN 1942 AT THE BATTLE OF MIDWAY. THIS SHIP SERVED IN WW II & VIETNAM & RECOVERED THE <u>APOLLO 8</u> ASTRONAUTS FROM THE SEA IN 1968.

C.P.O. MESS TRAY

PLEASE BUS YOUR TABLES, MATES.

THE MESS HALL IS OPEN TO THE PUBLIC IF ANY VETERANS WANT TO RELIVE THE COZY DINING ATMOSPHERE & GOURMET MEALS.

COMMISSION PENNANT

96

USS LAFFEY
(DD-724) 1944

DESTROYER — NAMED AFTER A CIVIL WAR MEDAL OF HONOR RECIPIENT. SERVED AT NORMANDY AND IN THE PACIFIC IN WWII AND IN THE KOREAN WAR.

INGHAM
(WHEC-35) 1936

COAST GUARD CUTTER — WWII & VIETNAM. A HIGHLY DECORATED SHIP.

USS CLAMAGORE (SS-343) 1945

SUBMARINE — ONE OF THE LAST DIESEL-POWERED SUBS.

WHEN SUBS ARE LOST AT SEA, THEY ARE SAID TO BE "STILL ON PATROL."

Shem Creek

HOME OF WORKING SHRIMP BOATS & CASUAL SEAFOOD RESTAURANTS WITH A VIEW OF CHARLESTON ACROSS THE COOPER RIVER.

The Wreck
OF THE
RICHARD & CHARLENE

A SEAFOOD RESTAURANT PARTLY INSIDE A LARGE WALK-IN FISH COOLER THAT WAS WRECKED BY THE TRAWLER <u>RICHARD & CHARLENE</u> DURING HURRICANE HUGO.

SHUCKED OYSTERS AT THE WRECK

98

Vickery's
RESTAURANT

WON FIRST PLACE—1996 CHARLESTON OYSTER FESTIVAL

Oyster Bisque

6-8 RAW WHOLE OYSTERS
1/2 CUP CORN
1/4 CUP GREEN ONIONS CHOPPED
1/4 CUP TOMATOES CHOPPED
2 OZ. WHITE WINE
6 OZ. HEAVY CREAM
1 OZ. GARLIC
SALT & PEPPER
TABASCO
WORCESTERSHIRE SAUCE

SAUTÉ CORN, GREEN ONIONS, & TOMATOES IN OLIVE OIL FOR 2-3 MINUTES. ADD GARLIC & COOK FOR 1 MINUTE. ADD WINE & REDUCE BY HALF. ADD CREAM & REDUCE. SEASON WITH SALT & PEPPER, TABASCO, WORCESTERSHIRE. ADD OYSTERS AND BRING TO A BOIL.

SERVE IMMEDIATELY.

BLACK-EYED PEA FRITTER

SHRIMP BOAT STUCK IN PLUFF MUD

Old Village
OF MT. PLEASANT

Settled in 1680, Mt. Pleasant was originally a farming community and a summer colony for planters looking for a cool, malaria-free environment.

CAROLINA
Pluff
Mud
BLACK BEAN
DRESSING

HYDRANGEAS & SUNFLOWERS

PLUFF MUD

IS GULLAH FOR THAT GOOEY,
SMELLY MUCK LEFT WHEN THE
TIDE GOES OUT IN THE
LOWCOUNTRY MARSHES.

ROCKLAND PLANTATION
PRODUCTS HAVE CREATED A
CLEVER BEAN DIP THAT LOOKS
(BUT DOESN'T SMELL) LIKE PLUFF MUD.

IT'S EASIER TO BUY A JAR THAN
TO FOLLOW THEIR RECIPE —

75 LBS. BLACK BEANS DRIED
50 LBS. SWEET ONIONS
150 CLOVES GARLIC
72 BAY LEAVES
11 GALLONS CHICKEN BROTH
75 JALOPEÑO PEPPERS
    — ETC.

WATERMELON

SUMMER SQUASH

OKRA

Creative planting places

at the Plantin Thyme Garden Center

"A Chapel of Ease"

THE CHURCH OF ENGLAND BUILT TEN CHAPELS IN THE "WILDERNESS" FOR THE EASE OF EARLY SETTLERS FAR FROM THE CITY.

CHRIST EPISCOPAL CHURCH 1726

COASTAL COTTAGE BUILT ON ORIGINAL HOME SITE c.1828

Snee Farm

CHARLES PINCKNEY NATIONAL HISTORIC SITE

BOUGHT BY COLONEL PINCKNEY IN 1754, SNEE FARM BECAME A 700-ACRE RICE, CATTLE, AND INDIGO PLANTATION. A DEFENDER OF SLAVERY, SON CHARLES PINCKNEY HAD 45 SLAVES IN 1787. ON HIS WAY INTO CHARLESTON IN 1791, GEORGE WASHINGTON STOPPED AND HAD BREAKFAST HERE.

TODAY, THERE ARE 28 ACRES LEFT.

Slave Inventory 1787	1787 English Pounds	(1995 $)
1. Cudjoe - Driver & Slaver	£120.00.00	$110,400
2. Wife Imba - Field Slave	80.00.00	73,600
3. Son - Wheelwright	60.00.00	55,200
4. Affy - House Wench	70.00.00	64,400

Charles Pinckney
1757–1824

CHARLES PINCKNEY GREW UP IN CHARLESTON. OVER HIS 67 YEARS, "CONSTITUTION CHARLEY" PUT TOGETHER QUITE A RESUMÉ:

- REVOLUTIONARY WAR PATRIOT
- DELEGATE TO THE CONSTITUTIONAL CONVENTION
- AUTHORED PARTS OF THE U.S. CONSTITUTION
- SIGNER OF THE U.S. CONSTITUTION
- GOVERNOR OF S.C. (4 TERMS)
- PRESIDENT— S.C. STATE CONSTITUTIONAL CONVENTION
- U.S. SENATOR
- CAMPAIGN MANAGER FOR THOMAS JEFFERSON
- AMBASSADOR TO SPAIN
- S.C. LEGISLATURE
- U.S. CONGRESSMAN

INDIGO

Eliza Lucas Pinckney*

THE FIRST WOMAN
AGRICULTURALIST
IN AMERICA.

As A BRITISH-EDUCATED 16-YEAR-OLD GIRL, ELIZA WAS PUT IN
CHARGE OF 3 LOWCOUNTRY PLANTATIONS WHILE HER FATHER
SERVED AS LT. GOVERNOR IN ANTIGUA. AT 22, SHE MARRIED
WIDOWER CHIEF JUSTICE PINCKNEY. IN 1739, SHE WAS THE
FIRST TO SUCCESSFULLY PLANT INDIGO IN AMERICA AND DEVELOP
A LUCRATIVE TRADE WITH EUROPE, SELLING THE BLUE INDIGO
DYE SHE PROCESSED. AT THE TIME, THE RICE MARKET WAS
SATURATED, AND INDIGO SAVED THE PLANTERS. THEN THE
REVOLUTIONARY WAR BROKE OUT AND THE INDIGO TRADE DIED.

(GEORGE WASHINGTON ASKED TO BE A PALL-
BEARER AT HER FUNERAL.)

RARE INDIGO "SEEDER"
(DRAWN AT
MIDDLETON PLACE)

* MOTHER OF
CHARLES COTES-
WORTH PINCKNEY,
SIGNER OF THE
CONSTITUTION.
AUNT TO CHARLES
PINCKNEY.

Making Indigo Dye

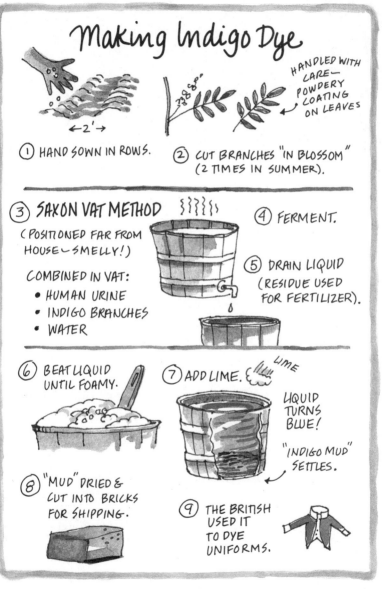

HANDLED WITH CARE — POWDERY COATING ON LEAVES

← 2' →

① HAND SOWN IN ROWS.

② CUT BRANCHES "IN BLOSSOM" (2 TIMES IN SUMMER).

③ SAXON VAT METHOD

(POSITIONED FAR FROM HOUSE — SMELLY!)

COMBINED IN VAT:
- HUMAN URINE
- INDIGO BRANCHES
- WATER

④ FERMENT.

⑤ DRAIN LIQUID (RESIDUE USED FOR FERTILIZER).

⑥ BEAT LIQUID UNTIL FOAMY.

⑦ ADD LIME. LIME

LIQUID TURNS BLUE!

"INDIGO MUD" SETTLES.

⑧ "MUD" DRIED & CUT INTO BRICKS FOR SHIPPING.

⑨ THE BRITISH USED IT TO DYE UNIFORMS.

Boone Hall Plantation

SAID TO BE THE MOST-PHOTOGRAPHED PLANTATION BECAUSE OF THE AVENUE OF OAKS LEADING TO THE HOUSE. THE LAND WAS GRANTED TO MAJ. JOHN BOONE IN THE 1680'S AND IT BECAME A COTTON AND BRICK MANUFACTURING PLANTATION. TODAY IT'S STILL AGRICULTURALLY ACTIVE.

ACTUAL SHOPPING LIST

1 negro girl	998 00
1 tea kettle	25
1 small pot	20
10 lb. sugar	1 50
1 days work by Sidney Vick —	50
shoeing one horse	50

BRICK SLAVE HOME

Boone Hall U-Picks
FIELDS & GROVES

U-PICK STRAWBERRIES "SIGN" ON HWY. 17

ARMLOADS OF ZINNIAS & YELLOW-FACE

SUNFLOWERS

PEACHES IN AN ORCHARD

LUSH TOMATOES

Sweetgrass Baskets

SLAVES BROUGHT BASKET-MAKING SKILLS TO THE PLANTATIONS FROM WEST AFRICA. WEAVING BASKETS WAS AN INTEGRAL PART OF DAILY WORK. SWEETGRASS BASKETS ARE NOW PART OF THE GULLAH CULTURE.

"These are sweetgrass baskets. Sweetgrass from the swamp, Bullrush from the marsh, Pine needles from the pine tree wrapping from the palmetto tree."

— ANNA'S CHANT

SADLY, SWEETGRASS IS BECOMING SCARCE & THE YOUNG AREN'T EAGER TO LEARN THE TRADITION.

DOROTHY'S CROSS-HANDLE BASKET

Sweetgrass SMELLS LIKE FRESHLY CUT HAY. GROWS NEAR THE OCEAN & MARSHLANDS.

Longleaf Pine NEEDLES USED FOR CONTRAST.

Leaves of Palm FROM PALMETTO OR CABBAGE PALM— A BINDER TO "SEW" COILS TOGETHER.

Split of White Oak MORE DURABLE THAN LEAVES OF PALM.

OLD SILVER SPOON HANDLE

Sewing "Bone" HOLDS SPACE OPEN SO BINDER CAN BE PULLED THROUGH.

SULLIVAN'S ISLAND

THE ISLAND FEELS LIKE A SUMMER GETAWAY, ALTHOUGH MANY LIVE HERE YEAR-ROUND. THERE ARE HOMES HERE FROM THE 1800'S, WHEN CHARLESTONIANS CAME TO ESCAPE THE "VIOLENT HEAT."

PLANTING A SUMMER GARDEN IN A JOHN BOAT

THE WINDOW BOXES OF SUMMER

AIRING THE HEIRLOOMS

DUNLEAVY'S PUB
ONE OF THE PLACES WHERE THE LOCALS GO

FORT MOULTRIE

NATIONAL MONUMENT
1776 – 1947

*F*ORT SULLIVAN WAS HASTILY BUILT FOR THE REVOLUTIONARY WAR USING PALMETTO TREE TRUNKS AND SAND. AFTER THE VICTORY OVER THE BRITISH, IT WAS RENAMED AFTER THE COMMANDER, COL. WILLIAM MOULTRIE.

SOUTH CAROLINA FLAG 1861

SILVER GORGET SYMBOL CAME FROM S.C. TROOP CAP.

STITCHED ON IN 3 PLACES

BLUE WAS THE UNIFORM COLOR.

PALMETTO TREE REPRE-SENTS VICTORY AT PALMETTO-LOG FORT.

CANNON SPONGE

"Don't let us fight without our color!"

SGT. WILLIAM JASPER RESCUING THE DOWNED FLAG

*C*HIEF OSCEOLA OF THE SEMINOLES WAS IMPRISONED HERE, BUT LOVED POSING FOR ARTISTS WHO REFERRED TO HIM AS "THE INDIAN ELEGANT". IN 1838 HE DRESSED IN HIS CALICO FINERY AND RED WAR PAINT, SHOOK HANDS ALL AROUND, THEN LAY DOWN & DIED AT 34. HE'S BURIED AT THE FORT.

FORT MOULTRIE
AND THE
Revolutionary War

JUNE 28 IS "CAROLINA DAY" IN SOUTH CAROLINA. IT WAS ON THAT DAY IN 1776 THAT THE BRITISH NAVY ATTACKED SULLIVAN'S ISLAND FOR 9 HOURS & LOST!

SURPRISINGLY, THE FORT'S FRESH-CUT PALMETTO-LOG WALLS WERE SPONGY SO THE SHOTS EITHER BOUNCED OFF OR BECAME EMBEDDED IN THE 16 FEET OF SAND BETWEEN THE DOUBLE WALLS.

ALTHOUGH COL. WM. MOULTRIE AND HIS TROOPS WERE OUTNUMBERED AND OUTGUNNED, THEY REPELLED THE BRITISH, WHO RETURNED SEVERAL YEARS LATER TO OCCUPY CHARLESTON.

"REV WAR" RE-ENACTORS ANNUALLY REPRESENT THE 2ND SOUTH CAROLINA REGIMENT STATIONED HERE ON JUNE 28, 1776.

18-lb. SIEGE GUN

— TAKES A CREW OF 16 TO FIRE IT EVERY 6 MINUTES.

WET CANNON SPONGE EXTINGUISHES ANY SPARKS IN THE BARREL.

WATER BUCKET TO WET SPONGE

18-lb. shot

IT TAKES 4 lbs. OF POWDER TO FIRE AN 18-POUND GUN — RE-ENACTORS USED ONLY ONE 1b. — AND BOY, WAS IT LOUD!

"MISS AMELIA" HAD TO HAND SEW HER DRESS, AS ALL LADIES DID AT THAT TIME.

RE-ENACTORS' WIVES BRING WATER TO MEN & CANNONS.

FORT MOULTRIE
AND THE
Civil War

BEDROLLED
FRESH-
FACED
YOUTH

MAJOR ROBERT ANDERSON AND HIS FEDERAL TROOPS WERE STATIONED HERE IN 1860, WHEN SOUTH CAROLINA SECEDED. HIS ORDERS WERE "TO HOLD POSSESSION OF THE FORTS IN THIS HARBOR."

FORT SUMTER WAS STRONGER & MORE STRATEGICALLY SITUATED THAN MOULTRIE. SO LATE ON DECEMBER 26, ANDERSON AND HIS MEN JAMMED THE GUNS AT MOULTRIE AND ROWED TO FORT SUMTER.

THE SOUTH SAW THE MOVE AS A BREACH OF FAITH AND AN ACT OF AGGRESSION. ON APRIL 12, 1861, THEY FIRED THE FIRST SHOT OF THE CIVIL WAR ON FORT SUMTER AND ANDERSON SURRENDERED 4 DAYS LATER.

CONFEDERATE & UNION RE-ENACTORS' GEAR

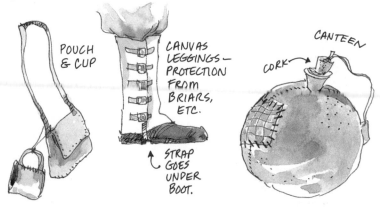

POUCH & CUP

CANVAS LEGGINGS — PROTECTION FROM BRIARS, ETC.

STRAP GOES UNDER BOOT.

CANTEEN

CORK

Otherwise Known As—

"War Between the States"

—◆—

"WAR OF NORTHERN AGGRESSION"

—◆—

"The War of Great Difficulty"

—◆—

"WAR FOR SOUTHERN INDEPENDENCE"

—◆—

"Recent Unpleasantness"

—◆—

"WAR OF THE REBELLION"

—◆—

"A Time of Great Unpleasantness"

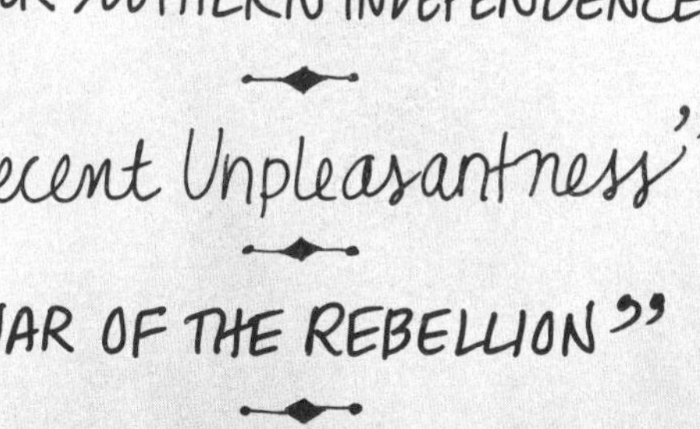

THE CONFEDERATE SUBMARINE BOAT
H·L·Hunley

HORACE L. HUNLEY

HORACE L. HUNLEY OF ALABAMA USED HIS LIFE'S SAVINGS TO BUILD THIS "TORPEDO BOAT," SENT HERE BY RAIL FROM MOBILE IN 1863.

ON FEBRUARY 17, 1864, THE HUNLEY ATTACKED THE UNION BLOCKADE SHIP HOUSATONIC, BECOMING THE FIRST SUBMARINE TO SINK AN ENEMY SHIP IN COMBAT. (AMERICA'S FIRST SUB, THE TURTLE, WAS UNSUCCESSFUL IN THE REVOLUTIONARY WAR.)

PROPELLED BY 8-MAN HAND CRANK

4'3"H × 3'10"W

39½' LONG

THE HUNLEY'S SAD HISTORY – 1863-1864

1. HUNLEY SWAMPED AT DOCKSIDE — 5 MEN LOST.
2. IT SANK IN TRAINING — 8 DIED, INCLUDING H.L. HUNLEY.
3. AFTER SINKING THE HOUSATONIC & KILLING 5 SAILORS, THE HUNLEY WAS LOST AT SEA WITH 8 MEN.

IN ALL, THE HUNLEY TOOK 26 LIVES.

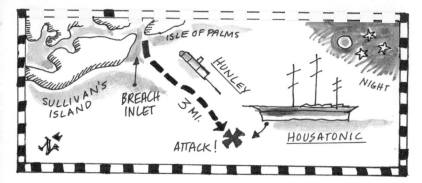

ISLE OF PALMS

HUNLEY

NIGHT

SULLIVAN'S ISLAND

BREACH INLET

3 MI.

ATTACK!

HOUSATONIC

THE ATTACK: FEBRUARY 17, 1864

1.
HOUSATONIC RAMMED BY SUB'S SPAR AT 4 KNOTS.

2.
TORPEDO LODGES IN SHIP.

3.
SUB BACKS OFF. PULLS DETONATING ROPE.

4.
TORPEDO EXPLODES. SHIP SINKS IN 5 MINUTES.

5.
HUNLEY SIGNALS SUCCESS VIA A BLUE LANTERN, THEN DISAPPEARS.

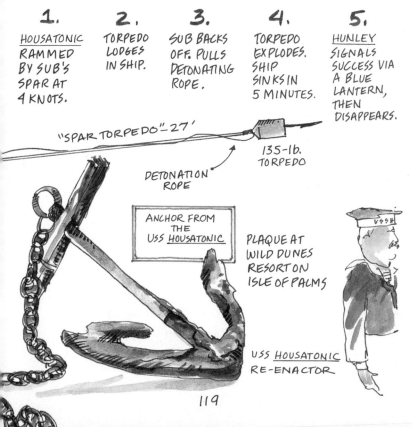

"SPAR TORPEDO" 27'

135-lb. TORPEDO

DETONATION ROPE

ANCHOR FROM THE USS HOUSATONIC

PLAQUE AT WILD DUNES RESORT ON ISLE OF PALMS

USS HOUSATONIC RE-ENACTOR

119

Raising the Hunley

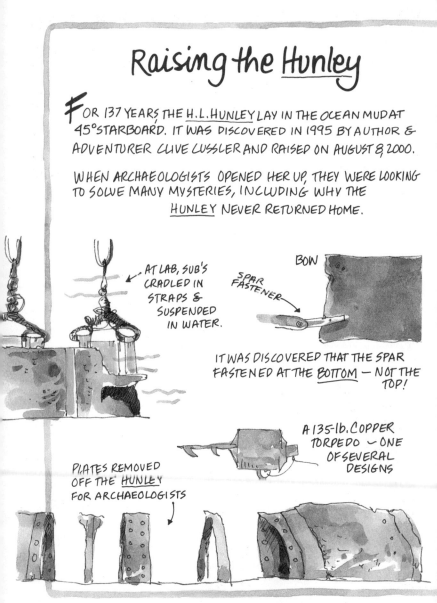

FOR 137 YEARS, THE H.L. HUNLEY LAY IN THE OCEAN MUD AT 45° STARBOARD. IT WAS DISCOVERED IN 1995 BY AUTHOR & ADVENTURER CLIVE CUSSLER AND RAISED ON AUGUST 8, 2000.

WHEN ARCHAEOLOGISTS OPENED HER UP, THEY WERE LOOKING TO SOLVE MANY MYSTERIES, INCLUDING WHY THE HUNLEY NEVER RETURNED HOME.

AT LAB, SUB'S CRADLED IN STRAPS & SUSPENDED IN WATER.

BOW

SPAR FASTENER

IT WAS DISCOVERED THAT THE SPAR FASTENED AT THE BOTTOM — NOT THE TOP!

A 135-lb. COPPER TORPEDO — ONE OF SEVERAL DESIGNS

PLATES REMOVED OFF THE HUNLEY FOR ARCHAEOLOGISTS

SPLIT PENCIL STUB

Some of the Discoveries

Shiloh.
April 6th 1862.
My Life Preserver.
G.E.D.

RTES OF AMERICA

ENTY D.

NAVY BUTTON
MADE OF RUBBER!
GOODYEAR HAD
AN 1851 PATENT.

3 BRASS BUTTONS
"A" IS FOR
ARTILLERY.

← GEORGE
WASHINGTON

BRASS I.D. TAG
BELONGING TO
EZRA CHAMBERLAIN—

A UNION SOLDIER!

—WHO HAD DIED ONE
YEAR EARLIER.
WHY WAS IT ON
THE HUNLEY?

PIPE BOWL
WITH A WAD OF
TOBACCO—EVEN
FOUND A
MATCHSTICK!

HUNLEY COMMANDER
LT. GEORGE DIXON
CARRIED A $20
GOLD PIECE WITH
HIM AS A GOOD
LUCK CHARM. IT
HAD SAVED HIS
LIFE AT SHILOH
WHEN A BULLET
HIT THE COIN &
STOPPED. HE THEN
HAD IT ENGRAVED
SINCE HIS LOVE,
QUEENIE BENNETT,
HAD FIRST GIVEN
IT TO HIM.

LEATHER SHOE—
VERY GOOPY.

CORKED
BUT EMPTY
MEDICINE BOTTLE?

END

WHITE FABRIC
OR PAPER?

ISLE OF PALMS

*T*HIS 5-MILE-LONG-BY-½-MILE-WIDE BARRIER ISLAND WAS ONCE OWNED BY ONE MAN, J. C. LONG. AFTER WWII, HE BEGAN SELLING PARCELS OF LAND. TODAY, HOMES LINE THE WIDE BEACH, WHICH LEAPS TO WILD DUNES RESORT, CAPPING THE NORTH END.

Sea Oats
Uniola paniculata, L.

SEA GRASSES AND DUNE FENCES HELP STRENGTHEN AND SUPPORT THE SAND DUNES, PREVENTING BEACH EROSION. SEA OATS ARE PROTECTED BY LAW.

PANICLES

SPIKELET SEED HEAD →

Island Life

DOLPHIN WATCHING

CHILD'S PLAY

ISLE OF PALMS MARINA

BEACH BUGGY

THE 13TH HOLE ON THE LINKS COURSE AT WILD DUNES RESORT

123

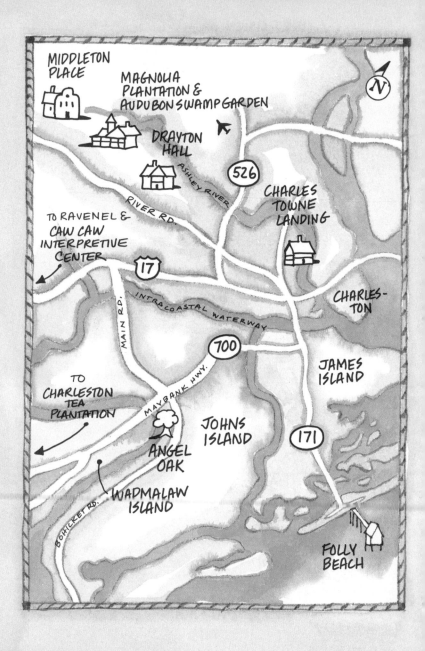

275–300-YEAR-OLD LIVE OAK AT DRAYTON HALL

CHAPTER 6

THE LOWCOUNTRY

WHEN THE <u>CAROLINA</u> AND HER PASSENGERS SET SAIL FROM ENGLAND TO COLONIZE CAROLINA, THEY STOPPED IN BARBADOS, WHERE THEY ENCOURAGED PLANTATION OWNERS AND OTHERS TO FOLLOW THEM TO THE NEW LAND.

PLANTERS FROM BARBADOS SOON JOINED THE CHARLES TOWNE COLONY. THEY AMASSED LAND FOR PLANTATIONS AND WERE DOMINANT IN COLONIAL GOVERNMENT AND THE ANGLICAN CHURCH. WITH THEIR LOVE FOR ELEGANCE AND A MERRY SOCIAL LIFE, THEY QUICKLY BECAME THE FIRST WEALTHY FAMILIES OF CHARLESTON.

"LAWD I GO WEH YOU WANT ME..."
—CAMP MEETING SONG

125

Charles Towne Landing

STATE HISTORIC SITE 1670

THE COLONISTS REACHED THE CAROLINA COAST & MET THE CASSIQUE (LEADER) OF THE KIAWAH INDIANS, WHO SUGGESTED THEY HEAD UP THE ASHLEY RIVER. IN APRIL 1670 THE <u>CAROLINA</u> LANDED HERE AT ALBEMARLE POINT WITH 93 PASSENGERS, 15 TONS OF BEER, 30 GALLONS OF BRANDY, AND BEADS FOR THE INDIANS.

THE POINT WAS RENAMED CHARLES TOWNE AFTER CHARLES II. THEY STAYED HERE 10 YEARS, THEN MOVED TO WHERE CHARLESTON IS TODAY.

CAPTAIN IN HIS SEA CLOTHES

SETTLERS FOUND NEW WILDLIFE, FROM MOSQUITOS TO BISON.

LATIN: Bison bison.

FRENCH: EXPLORERS CALLED THEM LES BOEUFS (OXEN).

ENGLISH: CHANGED IT TO LA BUFF.

NOW KNOWN AS **AMERICAN BUFFALO**

MOSCHETOES

THEY CALLED THEM "PESTIFEROUS GNATS."

THE HORRY-LUCAS HOME WAS BUILT IN ABOUT 1789 BUT DESTROYED BY FIRE. THE COLLEGE OF CHARLESTON FIELD SCHOOL WORKED ON THE EXCAVATION OF THE SITE AT CHARLES TOWNE LANDING.

TROWEL

THINGS THEY FOUND IN THE GROUND~

PORCELAIN SHARD~ (CHINESE IMPORT)

ACTUAL SIZE

ABORIGINAL SHARD

"ABORIGINAL" REFERS TO ARTIFACTS BEFORE EUROPEANS CAME. AFTER, THEY'RE KNOWN AS "HISTORICAL" ITEMS.

NAILS

STRIATIONS MADE FROM TURNING THIS KEY IN A LOCK

ANIMAL TOOTH

127

Drayton Hall 1738

GEORGIAN—
PALLADIAN
ARCHITECTURE

PLANES HAVE
TO GO ON
EITHER SIDE OF
THE HOUSE SO
IT WON'T
RATTLE.

PORTICO
INDICATES
PALLADIAN
ARCHITECTURE.

← ASHLEY RIVER

BUILT BY JOHN DRAYTON, WHO GREW UP ON THE MAGNOLIA PLANTATION.

REMARKABLY, THIS HOUSE HAS NEVER HAD PLUMBING, WATER, ELECTRICITY, OR GAS!

UNLIKE OTHER PLANTATION HOMES ALONG THE ASHLEY, THIS WAS SPARED FROM THE 1865 TORCHING BY UNION TROOPS. SOME SAY SMALLPOX FLAGS WERE POSTED AROUND THE HOUSE TO SCARE THE TROOPS AWAY.

LIGHT BRICKS FRAME DOORS & WINDOWS OUTSIDE.

EGG & DART MOLDING MEANS LIFE & DEATH.

Magnolia Plantation
& Gardens 1676

MAGNOLIA-ON-THE-ASHLEY WAS A WEDDING GIFT FROM STEPHEN FOX TO THOMAS DRAYTON JR. AND HIS WIFE, ANNE—ALL FROM BARBADOS. THE LAND HAS BEEN IN THE FAMILY SINCE 1676 AND THE DRAYTONS STILL LIVE THERE.

Dr. Drayton's Garden

STARTED IN THE 1680's, THIS IS THE OLDEST GARDEN IN AMERICA. IN THE 1800's THE REV. JOHN GRIMKE DRAYTON TURNED THE LAND INTO A VAST INFORMAL ENGLISH GARDEN FAMOUS FOR ITS AZALEAS AND CAMELLIAS.

NATIVE PINKSTER AZALEAS

129

LIKE ALL THE ASHLEY RIVER
PLANTATIONS, MAGNOLIA'S MAIN
CROP WAS RICE. THIS FAR
UPRIVER, THERE IS NO SALT IN
THE WATER SO THEY USED IT
TO FLOOD THE RICE FIELDS.

DIKES STILL KEEP OUT THE RIVER,
BUT AT MAGNOLIA, THE RICE
FIELDS ARE PERMANENTLY
FLOODED AS A WATERFOWL
REFUGE.

SNOWY
EGRET

HOOKED BILL
IS A CORMORANT.

STRAIGHT BILL
IS AN ANHINGA
OR SNAKE BIRD
OR BAT BIRD.

CATTAIL ISLANDS

LEASE TERNS

WHITE
IBIS

COOT

MOORHEN

GREAT
BLUE
HERON

John James Audubon
1785-1851

AUDUBON SKETCHED WILD LIFE AROUND CHARLESTON. AT MAGNOLIA, HE VISITED DR. DRAYTON AND COLLECTED AN ANHINGA SPECIMEN. IN TOWN, DR. JOHN BACHMAN, PASTOR OF ST. JOHN'S CHURCH, WAS A GOOD FRIEND WHO HELPED PRODUCE HIS BOOKS (LATER, AUDUBON'S TWO SONS MARRIED BACHMAN'S DAUGHTERS).

DETAIL OF
<u>ANHINGAS</u>
BY AUDUBON

<u>LONG-BILLED CURLEW</u> BY AUDUBON
(WITH THE CITY OF CHARLESTON IN THE BACKGROUND)

WITH APOLOGIES TO MR. AUDUBON

Audubon Swamp Garden
AT MAGNOLIA PLANTATION

FIDDLEHEADS (YOUNG FERNS)

WATER HYACINTH

POND CYPRESS & BALD CYPRESS

YOUNG CYPRESS "KNEES"

WOOD DUCK BOX

SEVERAL MOTHER WOOD DUCKS "DUMP" THEIR EGGS IN THE BOX. A FEW BABYSIT THE COLLECTION.

WATER LILY

DUCKWEED IS LIKE A CARPET ON THE WATER.

IT'S THE SMALLEST FLOWERING PLANT IN THE WORLD.

YELLOW-BELLIED TURTLES ON MAN-MADE RAMP

ALLIGATORS NEED SUN TO DIGEST FOOD.

First Flowers

MAGNOLIA
A PREHISTORIC TREE NATIVE ONLY TO
AMERICA AND ASIA. IT IS ONE OF
THE FIRST FLOWERING PLANTS TO
REPRODUCE BY INSECT
POLLINATION.

GARDENIA
DR. ALEXANDER GARDEN, A
CHARLESTON PHYSICIAN, FIRST
IMPORTED "CAPE JASMINE" FROM
SOUTH AFRICA IN ABOUT 1754. THE FLOWER
WAS RENAMED AFTER DR. GARDEN.

CAMELLIA (Camellia japonica)
FRENCH BOTANIST ANDRÉ MICHAUX
HAD A NURSERY NEAR CHARLESTON.
HE IMPORTED THE FIRST CAMELLIA
(REINE des FLEURS) & GAVE IT TO
MIDDLETON PLANTATION IN 1786.

AZALEA (Rhododendron)
SOME VARIETIES WERE NATIVE, BUT
REV. DRAYTON PLANTED Azalea indica
AT MAGNOLIA PLANTATION IN 1848.

133

MIDDLETON PLACE
1741

*T*HIS SOUTH FLANKER BUILDING IS ALL THAT'S LEFT AFTER THE MAIN HOUSE WAS BURNED DOWN BY UNION TROOPS IN 1865. THE 65-ACRE GARDEN PLANTED IN 1741 STILL REMAINS AND IS THE OLDEST LANDSCAPED GARDEN IN AMERICA.

OWNER HENRY MIDDLETON WAS PRESIDENT OF THE FIRST CONTINENTAL CONGRESS AND HIS SON ARTHUR WAS A SIGNER OF THE DECLARATION OF INDEPENDENCE.

ROYAL MUTE SWAN

134

THE STABLE YARDS AT MIDDLETON HAVE "LIVING EXHIBITS" SHOWING HOW WORK WAS DONE ON THIS PLANTATION. SHEEP PROVIDED THE WOOL & SLAVES DYED IT USING PLANTS AND INSECTS.

— DYED WOOLS —

MIMOSA TREE
ONLY THE LEAVES ARE USED FOR THE DYE.

COCHINEAL
A SCALE INSECT—
DYE MADE FROM DRIED
FEMALES. (60,000
MAKE 1 POUND OF
POWDER.)

RAGWEED
LEAVES & STEMS
USED FOR DYEING. COLOR
VARIES AS TO SOIL,
WATER, SEASON, ETC.

SPANISH MOSS
A MEMBER OF THE
PINEAPPLE FAMILY.

INDIGO
DYE MADE FROM LEAVES.

The Spoleto Finale
AT MIDDLETON PLACE

AN AFTERNOON &
NIGHT OF ENTERTAIN-
MENT, PICNICS, MUSIC, &
FIREWORKS ENDING THE
SPOLETO FESTIVAL.

PICNICS ARE ELEGANT
EXTRAVAGANZAS...

··· COVERING THE LAWN
OF MIDDLETON PLACE.

FOLDING CANVAS CHAIRS

PICNIC TRANSPORT

FLYER —— chief

A PICCOLO SPOLETO EVENT—AN OLD-TIME CAMP MEETING HELD AT THE FESTIVAL FINALE.

Mt. Zion Spiritual Singers

FOLLY BEACH

FOLLY BEACH
"THE EDGE OF AMERICA"

KING MACKEREL ARE CAUGHT OFF THE EDWIN S. TAYLOR FISHING PIER — MORE THAN 1000' LONG.

LIKE CHARLESTON, THIS BARRIER ISLAND BEACH COMMUNITY WAS DEVASTATED IN 1989 BY HURRICANE HUGO AND HAS SINCE BEEN REBUILT.

↖ ATTORNEYS WITH A SENSE OF HUMOR!

Angel Oak

THOUGHT TO BE OVER 1,400 YEARS OLD, THIS LIVE OAK WAS NAMED AFTER JUSTIS ANGEL WHO MARRIED MARTHA WAIGHT IN 1810 (THE WAIGHT FAMILY HAD OWNED THE SITE SINCE 1717). THE TREE & PARK ARE NOW OWNED BY THE CITY OF CHARLESTON.

LIMBS GROW AT RIGHT ANGLES TO THE TRUNK — WERE USED FOR SHIP-BUILDING.

HOME TO BIG ANTS

RESURRECTION FERN — TURNS FROM BROWN TO GREEN WITH RAIN.

KNOTHOLES TRAP WATER FOR INSECTS.

SPANISH MOSS GETS NUTRIENTS FROM AIR.

TWISTED GRAIN ADDED STRENGTH FOR SHIP-BUILDING.

André Michaux 1746-1802

"THE KING'S BOTANIST" WAS SENT TO AMERICA IN 1785 BY LOUIS XVI TO CATALOG & COLLECT PLANTS AND TREES FOR THE ROYAL NURSERIES IN FRANCE. MICHAUX STARTED A NURSERY OUTSIDE CHARLESTON (WHERE THE AIRPORT IS NOW) AND WAS THE FIRST TO INTRODUCE MANY PLANTS TO AMERICA VIA CHARLESTON. BESIDES THE CAMELLIA & SOME AZALEAS, HE ALSO IMPORTED —

Melia azedarach "PERSIAN LILAC"

Akebia quinata "CHOCOLATE VINE"

Camellia sinensis "TEA PLANT"

Albizia julibrissin "MIMOSA"

Lagerstroemia "CREPE MYRTLE"

Ginkgo biloba "GOLDEN FOSSIL TREE"

Osmanthus fragrans "SWEET OLIVE"

CHARLESTON TEA PLANTATION
History

1799– FRENCH BOTANIST ANDRÉ MICHAUX INTRODUCED THE FIRST TEA PLANTS TO MIDDLETON PLACE, CHARLESTON.

1888– PINEHURST TEA PLANTATION PROSPERED IN SUMMERVILLE, SOUTH CAROLINA, UNTIL ITS OWNER DIED.

1963– THOMAS J. LIPTON, INC., PLANTED SOME OF PINEHURST'S ORIGINAL TEA BUSHES HERE AT THEIR RESEARCH STATION.

1987– HORTICULTURALIST MACK FLEMING & TEA TASTER WILLIAM BARCLAY HALL BOUGHT THE PROPERTY FROM LIPTON & NOW PRODUCE

AMERICAN CLASSIC TEA
THE ONLY TEA GROWN IN AMERICA.

SPECIAL HARVESTER TAKES NEW LEAVES OFF THE TOPS OF BUSHES.

Sweet Tea
A Southern Comfort!

INGREDIENTS:

1 "HEAPING" CUP OF SUGAR
2 QUARTS OF COLD WATER
JUICE OF TWO LEMONS
5 REGULAR TEA BAGS
(ADD MORE BAGS
  FOR STRONGER TEA)

DIRECTIONS:

COMBINE SUGAR, WATER, AND LEMON JUICE IN A LARGE
SAUCEPAN. BRING TO A BOIL OVER HIGH HEAT,
STIRRING FREQUENTLY. REMOVE FROM HEAT, ADD
THE TEA BAGS, COVER THE PAN, AND STEEP FOR 20
MINUTES. REMOVE TEA BAGS AND POUR INTO
LARGE PITCHER.   CHILL AND SERVE. *

* RECIPE
COMPLIMENTS
OF THE S.C
SMILES GUIDE

Caw Caw
INTERPRETIVE CENTER

THIS EDUCATIONAL CENTER, SURROUNDED BY THE CAW CAW SWAMP, ENCOMPASSES SEVERAL FORMER RICE PLANTATIONS.

SLAVES FROM THE RICE-GROWING REGIONS OF AFRICA'S WEST COAST WERE VALUED FOR THEIR AGRICULTURAL AND TECHNICAL SKILLS. WITH THEIR EXPERIENCE AND LABOR, RICE BECAME SO PROFITABLE IT WAS CALLED "CAROLINA GOLD".

MULE BOOT
HELPED MULES SLOG THROUGH MUDDY RICE FIELDS.

SLAVES CLEARED SWAMPS FOR RICE FIELDS.

RICE TRUNK
REGULATED WATER IN & OUT OF RICE FIELDS.

143

"Carolina Gold"
PLANTING & HARVESTING RICE

EARLY SPRING
SEEDS SOWN BEFORE "RICE BIRDS" (BOBOLINK) MIGRATE THROUGH HERE LOOKING FOR FOOD.

HOEING WEEDS IN THE MUD WAS A CONSTANT TASK.

LATE SUMMER: WATER FLOODS FIELDS. THEN WHEN SEED HEADS BEND DOWN, FIELDS ARE DRAINED DRY & THE RICE IS CUT WITH RICE HOOKS.

A DAY AFTER HARVESTING, RICE IS BUNDLED INTO SHEAVES & STACKED FOR DRYING.

RICE IS THRESHED, THEN WINNOWED IN A FANNA BASKET.

MORTAR & PESTLE — USED TO POUND RICE

ROUND END CRACKS THE HULL.

POINTED END TAKES BRAN OFF & POLISHES IT.

SABAL PALM IN BLOOM, *Sabal palmetto*

STATE TREE OF SOUTH CAROLINA

Appendix

Points of Interest in Charleston and Surrounding Areas

Aiken-Rhett House
48 Elizabeth Street
843-723-1159

Alice's Fine Foods
468-470 King Street
843-853-9366

American Military Museum
360 Concord Street
843-723-9620

Angel Oak
3688 Angel Oak Road
Johns Island
843-559-3496

Ashley Hall
172 Rutledge Avenue
843-722-4088

Audubon Swamp Garden at
   Magnolia Plantation
3550 Ashley River Road
843-571-1266/800-367-3517

Avery Research Center
125 Bull Street
843-953-7608

Boone Hall Plantation
1235 Long Point Road
Mount Pleasant
843-884-4371

Burbage's Grocery
157 Broad Street
843-723-4054

Cabbage Row (aka Catfish Row)
89-91 Church Street

Cathedral of St. Luke and St. Paul
126 Coming Street
843-722-7345

Caw Caw Interpretive Center
5200 Savannah Highway
Ravenel
843-889-8898

Central Station
46 ½ Wentworth Street
843-720-1981

Charles Towne Landing State
   Historic Site
1500 Old Towne Road
843-852-4200

Charleston City Hall
80 Broad Street
843-577-6970

Charleston County Historic
    Courthouse
84 Broad Street
843-958-4099

Charleston Farmers Market
Marion Square
843-724-7309

The Charleston Museum
360 Meeting Street
843-722-2996

Charleston Tea Plantation
6617 Maybank Highway
Wadmalaw Island
1-800-443-5987

Charleston Visitor Reception and
    Transportation Center
375 Meeting Street
843-853-8000, 800-868-8118

Christ Episcopal Church
2304 U.S. Highway 17 N.
Mt. Pleasant
843-884-9090

Circular Congregational Church
150 Meeting Street
843-577-6400

The Citadel
171 Moultrie Street
843-953-5000

The Citadel Museum
171 Moultrie Street
843-953-6846

College of Charleston
66 George Street
843-953-5507

The Confederate Home
60-64 Broad Street

The DeSaussure House
1 East Battery

Dock Street Theatre
135 Church Street
843-720-3968

Drayton Hall
3380 Ashley River Road
843-766-0188

Dunleavy's Pub
2213-B Middle Street
Sullivan's Island
843-883-9646

Edmonston-Alston House
21 East Battery
843-722-7171

Edwin S. Taylor Fishing Pier
101 E. Arctic
Folly Beach
843-588-3474

Eighty-Two Church
108 Church Street
843-723-7511/800-377-1282

82 Queen
82 Queen Street
843-723-7591

Emanuel AME Church
110 Calhoun
843-722-2561

Festival of Houses and Gardens
Historic Charleston Foundation
40 East Bay Street
843-722-3405

Fort Moultrie
1214 W. Middle Street
Sullivan's Island
843-883-3123

Fort Sumter Visitor Education &
  Tour Boat Facility
Liberty Square
843-883-3123

French Huguenot Church
136 Church Street
843-722-4385

Gibbes Museum of Art
135 Meeting Street
843-722-2706

Jonathon Green
316 Morgan Road
Naples, FL
239-775-9999

Gullah Tours by Alphonso Brown
9 Trachelle Lane
843-763-7551

The Heyward-Washington House
87 Church Street
843-722-0354

Historic Charleston Foundation
40 East Bay Street
843-723-1623

H.L. *Hunley* at the Warren Lasch
  Conservation Center
1250 Supply Street, Bldg. 255
N. Charleston
843-722-2333 (Friends of the
  Hunley)

Hominy Grill
207 Rutledge
843-937-0930

Hyman's Seafood
215 Meeting Street
843-723-6000

Isle of Palms Marina
50 41st Avenue
Isle of Palms
843-886-0209

Johnson & Wales
701 East Bay Street
843-727-3000/800-868-1522

Joseph Manigault House
350 Meeting Street
843-723-2926

The Joseph P. Riley Jr. Park
 ("The Joe")
360 Fishburne Street
843-723-7241

Kahal Kadosh Beth Elohim
90 Hasell Street
843-723-1090

Magnolias
185 East Bay Street
843-577-7771

Magnolia Plantation & Gardens
3550 Ashley River Road
843-571-1266/800-367-3517

Middleton Place
4300 Ashley River Road
843-556-6020

Miles Brewton House
27 King Street

Miss Nicki's Olde Time Photos
30 Vendue Range
843-723-5550

Moja Arts Festival
843-724-7305

Moo Roo
316 King Street
843-534-2233

Mt. Zion Spiritual Singers
c/o AME Church
8419 Willtown Road
Hollywood
843-889-6275

Nathaniel Russell House
51 Meeting Street
843-724-8481

Office of Cultural Affairs
133 Church Street
843-724-7305

The Old Exchange & Provost
 Dungeon
122 East Bay Street
843-727-2165

Old Slave Mart Museum
6 Chalmers Street
843-724-3726

Olde Towne Carriage Company
20 Anson Street
843-722-1315

Palmetto Carriage Works, Ltd.
40 North Market Street
843-723-8145

Patriots Point
40 Patriots Point Road
Mt. Pleasant
843-884-2727

Piccolo Spoleto Festival
843-724-7305

Plantin Thyme Garden Center
1147 Bowman Road
Mount Pleasant
843-881-0867

Postal History Museum
83 Broad Street
843-577-0690

The Preservation Society of
   Charleston
147 King Street
843-722-4630

Rainbow Row
79-107 East Bay Street

Rockland Plantation Products
P.O. Box 363
Mt. Pleasant, SC 29465
843-729-6609

Philip Simmons
   Home and Forge
   30 ½ Blake Street

   Philip Simmons Foundation,
      Inc.
   P.O. Box 21585
   Charleston, SC 29413-1585
   843-723-8018

   Garden
   91 Anson Street
   843-723-8018

Slightly North of Broad
192 East Bay Street
843-723-3424

Snee Farm Charles Pinckney
   National Historic Site
1254 Longpoint Road
Mt. Pleasant
843-881-5516

South Carolina Aquarium
100 Aquarium Wharf
843-577-3474

Southeastern Wildlife Exposition
211 Meeting Street
843-723-1748

Spirit of South Carolina
South Carolina Maritime Heritage
    Foundation
843-860-0999

Spoleto Festival
843-579-3100

St. John's Lutheran Church
10 Archdale Street
843-723-2426

St. Michael's Episcopal Church
80 Meeting Street
843-723-0603

St. Philip's Episcopal Church
146 Church Street
843-722-7734

Two Meeting Street Inn
2 Meeting Street
843-723-7322

Unitarian Church
6 Archdale Street
843-723-4617

Vendue Inn
19 Vendue Range
843-577-7970

Vickery's Restaurant
1313 Shrimp Boat Lane
Mt. Pleasant
843-884-4440

Mrs. Whaley's Garden
58 Church Street

Wild Dunes Resort
5757 Palm Boulevard
Isle of Palms
843-886-2113

The Wreck of the *Richard*
    and Charlene
106 Haddrell Street
Mt. Pleasant
843-884-0052

acknowledgments

A heartfelt thank you to editor Antonia Fusco and publisher Elisabeth Scharlatt for their support and encouragement.

Thank you to my Charleston connections: Nicki Clendening's long lists of "things to do" and Shannon Ravenel's local insights were priceless. Becky Hollingsworth was our personal introductory tour guide and gave us shelter during our stay in Charleston. Sarah Ragsdale of Explore Charleston Tours was a wealth of expert and eclectic information, and I am grateful for her help and humor.

Thank you to some new friends: The lovely Virginia Neyle and Sallie Simons gave me a glimpse of a genteel Charleston. Rosalea Donahue was a fast friend and an enthusiastic fact finder. Deedie Cooper literally gave us the cook's tour of markets and Lowcountry cooking. My long-time friend Patsy Graham discovered the Charleston Bonnet for me.

Thank you to the artists who were so gracious with their time: Master blacksmith Philip Simmons and his nephew Carlton, seamstress Jean Hutchinson, and artist Jonathon Green.

Thank you to the historians and experts who know it all: Alphonso Brown of Gullah Tours, Michael Huggins at City Hall, Rick Hatcher at Ft. Moultrie, Ranger Bill Martin at Snee Farm, Shawn Halifax at Caw Caw Interpretive Center, Kellen Butler at Friends of the *Hunley*, Dr. Steve Ewing at Patriots Point, Deborah Wright at Avery Research Center.

Thank you to Mayor Joseph P. Riley Jr., who took time out of his incredibly busy schedule to meet with me.

Just so I don't miss anyone, a sincere Southern thank you to all those Charlestonians who graciously shared their recipes; let me linger in their stores, museums, places of worship, libraries, and restaurants; and reviewed the manuscript pages.

Finally, a loving thank you to my mother, Gail, and to my patient husband, Paul, who kept thinking this book was done when it wasn't.

WOOD STORK

Index